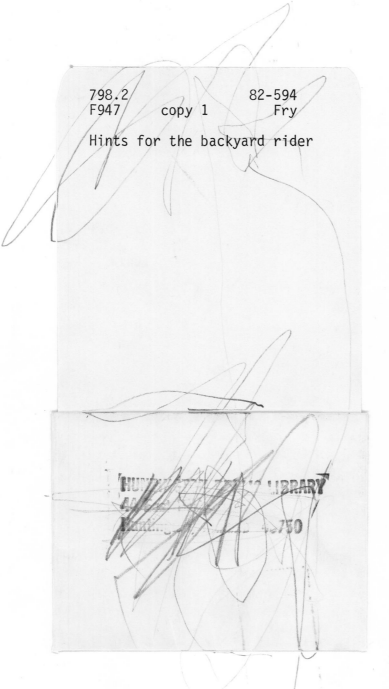

HINTS FOR THE BACKYARD RIDER

HINTS FOR THE BACKYARD RIDER

Patricia L. Fry

South Brunswick and New York:
A. S. Barnes and Company
London: Thomas Yoseloff Ltd

© 1978 by A. S. Barnes and Co., Inc.

A. S. Barnes and Co., Inc.
Cranbury, New Jersey 08512

Thomas Yoseloff Ltd
Magdalen House
136-148 Tooley Street
London SE1 2TT, England

Library of Congress Cataloging in Publication Data

Fry, Patricia L., 1940-
    Hints for the backyard rider.

    Includes index.
    1.   Horses.   2.   Horsemanship.   I.   Title.
SF285.F78   636.1   77-84568
ISBN 0-498-02166-1
ISBN 0-498-02305-2 pbk.

Illustrations by V. Lee Swift.
Photographs by the author.

PRINTED IN THE UNITED STATES OF AMERICA

*This book is dedicated
to the memory of my first backyard horse,
Tammy.*

CONTENTS

ACKNOWLEDGMENTS

I wish to thank the following people for their assistance and support during the preparation of this book:

My husband, Marty, for his encouragement.

My children, Terri, Penny, and Marti, for their patience and help.

George Kosten, for his advice and helpful criticism.

Carol Kosten, for her valuable array of knowledge.

Drs. John Bee and John Lyons, veterinarians, for editing chapter four.

Lynn Roberts, for her expert advice in the photographic area.

Fred Volz, for his aid in editing the book.

Gini Swift for her excellent drawings.

And the many horsepeople from the Ojai Valley, who gave of their knowledge and time.

HINTS FOR THE BACKYARD RIDER

1 WHAT IS A HORSE?

The horse has been at man's side throughout many centuries, demonstrating the nobility and strength he has always symbolized. Even though the age of the machine forced the horse out to pasture, this ancient companion of man has never been as loved and admired as he is today.

Horsemanship is one of the fastest growing sports in America. It offers people yet another way of getting down to the basics of nature. A horse has a way of helping his rider forget the pressures and problems of everyday life in the mechanical world, providing relief from the world of concrete and asphalt.

But what about the horse owner? What is it that causes people to yearn for their own horse? Is it the personality and beauty of this great animal? Is it that we want to dominate a creature of such size and strength? Perhaps it is the romance of the horse . . . his historical significance. Whatever the reasons, the horse no longer must toil for his keep. He is now an object of pleasure.

The horse of today opens the gate to many worlds for his owner. There are trail rides, shows, horse and buggy social organizations, endurance rides, fox hunts, racing, roping, and even drill teams and parades. Pleasure riding is another popular form that this recreation encompasses.

We are constantly made aware of the importance of exercise for our health. Horseback riding fills this need. Riding tightens muscles, firms flab, and burns up calories as fast as walking, bowling, and many other forms of exercise. Think back to the first time that you rode.

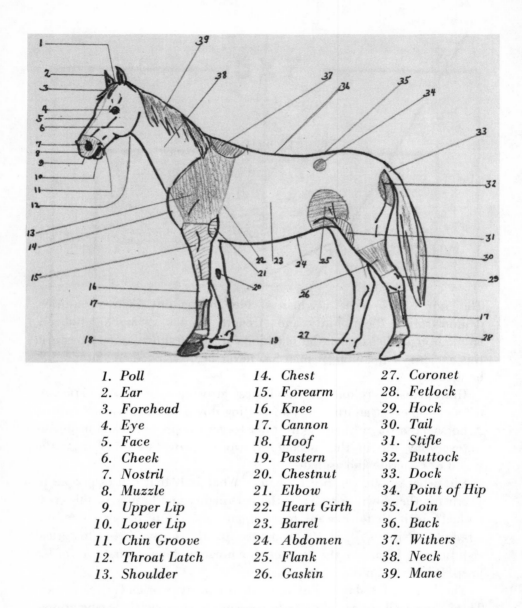

1. Poll	14. Chest	27. Coronet
2. Ear	15. Forearm	28. Fetlock
3. Forehead	16. Knee	29. Hock
4. Eye	17. Cannon	30. Tail
5. Face	18. Hoof	31. Stifle
6. Cheek	19. Pastern	32. Buttock
7. Nostril	20. Chestnut	33. Dock
8. Muzzle	21. Elbow	34. Point of Hip
9. Upper Lip	22. Heart Girth	35. Loin
10. Lower Lip	23. Barrel	36. Back
11. Chin Groove	24. Abdomen	37. Withers
12. Throat Latch	25. Flank	38. Neck
13. Shoulder	26. Gaskin	39. Mane

Remember how sore you were? That is because you were using muscles that are ordinarily neglected.

Getting to know a variety of horses is a good idea for anyone who is interested in having his own. Rent horses from riding stables; talk to acquaintances who have horses; write to the county agriculture agent for help in contacting horse groups in your area; participate in these clubs' activities. These generally include horse show playdays, trail rides, educational clinics, informative speakers, and such. You needn't

14

This backyard gets trimmed regularly.

have a horse to participate in these events. Just being around horses, and the people who love and know them, can help you to learn more about this animal. Remember to be open to this invaluable array of knowledge.

Each horse is an individual. Each has a personality unique to any other. People who have managed dogs and cats and who can relate well to these smaller animals will probably find the horse a most enjoyable companion. Although a very different creature than the household pet, the horse has qualities that a devoted human friend will benefit from.

As there are certain signs that tell you when your dog is happy or irritated, so it is with the horse. His ears generally show his state of mind. If they are forward and his head is up and eyes are wide open, he is alert and inquisitive. He may be snorting and moving backwards, which indicates he is suspicious or frightened. When the ears are laid back against his head, he is displaying his anger. The tail might swish rapidly from side to side and he may paw the ground to further demonstrate anger or impatience.

Happiness, too, can be made obvious by the horse. He will playfully run, buck, and kick up his heels when showing an extreme spurt of joy. We've all seen a performance of this type in an open field. A low, throaty nicker implies pleasure. The sound is most commonly heard at feeding time. Some horses are genuinely affectionate. However, the

15

friendly nuzzling we might get from a horse is not usually a sign of love at all but a need to be scratched where the sweat has dried behind his ears.

These and other characteristics mentioned in this book are general. Although all horses use the same signs to show their inner feelings, it · takes a wide range of events to provoke these reactions. To put it in simple terms: while some dogs wag their tails at the sight of their leash, others may run and hide. So it is with horses; no two will always react in an identical manner to the same situation.

The horse, as large as he is, can be easily frightened. A strange noise, an object of an unusual size or shape, or a fluttering leaf can turn him into a quivering coward. His normal reaction to such a scare is to flee. His greatest means of protection through the years has been his legs, and the ability to use them to get far from the source of danger. Many a gentle, level-headed horse has caused a dangerous situation when terrified.

Always remember that we are responsible for the well-being and safety of these dependent creatures.

You may have heard people refer to a fairly large horse as a "pony." This is usually incorrect. The difference between a horse and a pony is size. If he is over 58" in height (or 14.2 hands), he is a horse, less than that a pony.

The height of a horse is measured from the highest point at the

Many young girls' dreams begin unexpectedly on a drive in the country.

16

Getting acquainted.

withers (top of the shoulders) to the ground. One hand equals four inches, the average width of a man's hand. A 15-hand horse stands sixty inches tall. Additional inches are put after a decimal point. For instance, 16.2 hands is equal to 16 hands plus 2 inches (or fingers).

A grown male horse is called a stallion, unless he is castrated or gelded. Then he is a gelding. A mature female horse is called a mare. A

Lawrence Outland, Santa Paula, California, finds pleasure in driving Phyllis and Phoebe rather than riding them.

foal is a horse under one year old. A filly is a female horse up to three years old, and a colt is a male horse up to three years of age.

A purebred horse is one that is registered with a recognized horse association. The word *Thoroughbred* refers to a particular breed of horse. When a person uses the term *thoroughbred Arabian* or *thoroughbred dog,* he is incorrect. He should say *purebred Arabian* or *purebred German Shepherd. Grade* is the term given a horse with unknown ancestry. An unregistered horse having characteristics of one of the recognized breeds may be considered a Quarter-type mare or an Arabian-type gelding, but these, too, are grade horses.

Listed here are a few characteristics and identifying marks of some of the more well-known breeds in America today.

ARABIAN: Known also as an Arab, this is the oldest breed of what is known as improved livestock. Characteristics include a dished face, short ears, large eyes, and fine muzzle. The neck is well arched and the tail is carried in a natural arch of its own. The Arabian is smaller than most other breeds of horses. An extremely hardy animal, he is one of the soundest. His endurance abilities make him a constant winner in long, rugged, timed trail events. He can also be used for polo. The colors you'll find predominant in this breed are bay, gray, and chestnut. Black, brown, and white are seen occasionally.

18

APPALOOSA: This striking animal is associated with the Nez Perce Indians who lived in the northwest states of Oregon, Washington, and Idaho. Color is the distinguishing characteristic here; it varies from a pale red roan with slight frosting over the hips to coal black with huge peacock spots of whites and grays. His eyes are encircled by a white sclera, much like the human eye. The skin around the nostrils, lips, and under the tail is mottled or parti-colored. The hooves show wide stripes of black and white. The mane and tail are generally thin and short. You may hear people refer to a spotted horse such as this as an "Appy" or an "Ap." Although not incorrect, many Appaloosa fans do not like to hear these nicknames.

MORGAN: The Morgan is a popular horse because of his endurance and vigor. He has a particularly proud head carriage and a well-crested neck. He is a pleasure to his owners whether they participate in trail rides or they show in either English or Western classes.

QUARTER HORSE: A versatile, well-muscled animal. The Quarter Horse head is characterized by small ears and a large jaw. Their quiet, gentle disposition has made this breed the most popular one in America today. Pleasure riding, roping, cutting, and even jumping are some of the things for which these horses are used. Ranch work is what they were bred for. They are sure-footed, clever, and they can start and stop with extreme precision.

The friendship of this boy and his pony develops through times of play.

THOROUGHBRED: This horse is considerably taller than those I have mentioned. They are most usually 15.3 hands or taller. Selected primarily for racing, these horses are also hunters and jumpers.

COLOR BREEDS

AMERICAN ALBINO: A snow-white coat, pink skin, and dark blue or brown eyes are points typical to an Albino.

PALOMINO: This horse is usually the color of newly minted gold, with varying shades lighter and darker. His mane and tail are white, silver, or ivory. A strikingly lovely horse, he is seen often in parades, as well as in any other form of showing or using horses.

PINTO: Indians have termed this horse the typical "Indian Pony." Large spots of white and a dark color, such as brown, black, dun, sorrel, or roan, cover his body. Glass (or blue) eyes are a common trait of this horse.

PAINT: A horse that has pinto coloring and either Thoroughbred or Quarter Horse breeding can be registered in the Paint Association.

Ponies and horses can pull more weight than they can carry.

PONY BREEDS

PONY OF AMERICA: The P.O.A., as it is also known, cannot be under 46" or over 54" tall. He has Appaloosa coloring and features with the body type of a miniature cross between a Quarter Horse and an Arabian. In performance classes he must be ridden by youths no older than seventeen years of age.

SHETLAND PONY: Maximum height for registration of this tiny model is 46" (11.2 hands). He will weigh from 250 to 500 pounds. Requiring little feed, these ponies tend to founder on pasture. Coats are long and shaggy, especially in the winter. Shetland Ponies come in almost any color.

WELSH PONY: This larger pony is for children who have outgrown the Shetland. The Welsh goes up to 14 hands in height.

For more information on these and other horse breeds, contact the proper organization as listed below.

American Albino Association
P.O. Box 79
Crabtree, Oregon 97335

American Quarter Horse Association
Box 200
Amarillo, Texas 79105

American Shetland Pony Club
P.O. Box 1250
Lafayette, Indiana 47902

American Hackney Horse Society
Room 725
527 Madison Ave.
New York, New York 10022

American Saddle Horse Breeders
929 So. 4th St.
Louisville, Ky. 40203

Arabian Horse Club
Registry of American
332 Michigan Ave.
Chicago, Ill. 60604

The Palomino Horse Assn., Inc.
Box 446
Chatsworth, Calif. 91311

Pinto Horse Assn. of America
P.O. Box 3984
San Diego, Calif. 92103

Pony of the Americas Club
P.O. Box 1447
Mason City, Iowa 50401

Tennessee Walking Horse
Breeders and Exhibitors
Assn. of America
Box 286
Lewisburg, Tenn. 37091

Appaloosa Horse Club
Box 403
Moscow, Idaho 83843

Welsh Pony Society of America
P.O. Box 419
Unionville, Pa. 19375

Morgan Horse Club
P.O. Box 2157
Bishop's Corner Ranch
West Hartford, Conn. 06117

American Paint Horse Assn.
P.O. Box 12487
Fort Worth, Texas 17116

Palomino Horse Breeders of America
Box 249
Mineral Wells, Texas 76067

Standardbred Trotting Assn.
750 Michigan Ave.
Columbus, Ohio 43215

Thoroughbred, The Jockey Club
300 Park Ave.
New York, New York 10022

COLORS

BAY: A body color varying from light golden to reddish brown. The points (mane, tail, and lower legs) are black.

BLOOD BAY: The same as a bay, but the body color is dark red.

BLACK: The entire body is black without any light areas.

BROWN: This horse can be almost black, but you will notice light areas around the muzzle, eyes, and on the rear. The black points, as in a bay horse, are also present.

BUCKSKIN: A yellow or golden body color with black points.

CHESTNUT: A reddish brown body color of varying shades with the mane and tail the same shade. Mane and tail can be lighter, but never black.

SORREL: A light yellowish red to a rich mahogany.

DUN: A yellow color ranging from a light cream to Palomino gold. Mane and tail may be black, brown, red, yellow, or mixed. Often a dorsal stripe appears down the back.

GRAY: This animal will vary from a dark steel-gray to a light silver-gray. The shade is established by a composition of white and black hairs throughout the coat. Most gray horses are born black.

Star	*Strip*	*Snip*
Bald	*Blaze*	*Star/Strip/Snip*

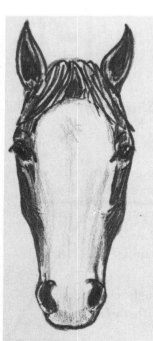  

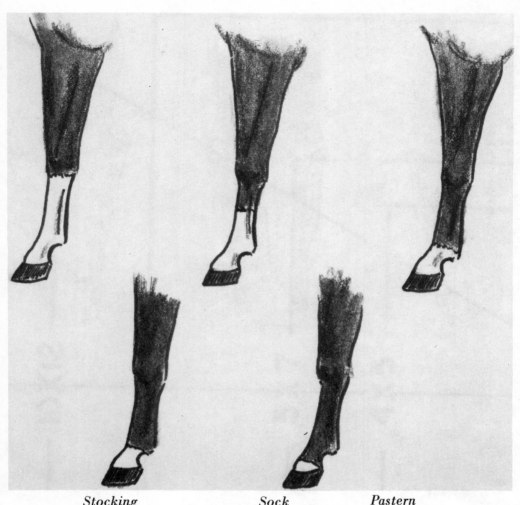

Stocking   *Sock*   *Pastern*

1/2 Pastern   *Coronet*

GRULLA: This is a Spanish word for "mouse." The grulla horse is a mousey grey-brown with black points and a black line down the back.

PALOMINO: Golden body color that varies from copper to light gold.

ROAN: White hairs intermingle with darker colors to cause a roan horse. Red roan is white and bay, strawberry roan is white and chestnut, blue roan is white with brown or black.

WHITE: Sometimes a light-colored Palomino is wrongly considered a white horse. A white horse does not change colors with the seasons as other horses tend to do.

HEAD AND LEG MARKINGS

STAR: A white mark of varying sizes on the forehead.

SNIP: A white mark between the nostrils.

STRIP: A narrow vertical white mark running down the center of the face.

BLAZE: A white mark down the face that is broader than the strip.

BALD: White that covers most of the horse's face, usually extending to the outsides of the eyes.

These markings are sometimes found in combinations. For instance, a horse might have a short blaze and a snip, or a star and a snip.

CORONET: A narrow white stripe around the area just above the hoof.

HALF-PASTERN: A white area from the hoof, halfway up to the pastern.

PASTERN: The same mark as the half-pastern but extending up to the fetlock.

SOCK: The white of a sock extends halfway up to the cannon bone.

STOCKING: White that reaches almost to the hock and knee.

2 THE RIGHT HORSE FOR YOU

If you don't already have a horse, you are probably considering buying one, or you wouldn't be reading this book. Most people make a mistake on the purchase of their first horse. They are so eager to fill their corral that they buy the first horse that nuzzles them. Perhaps you can't resist that big Pinto that reminds you of the horse you rode at "Y" camp ten years ago, or the friendly bay that keeps trying to take bites of your straw hat. But you're better off in the long run if you put restraint on your heart and use your head.

First of all, be really sure that you want your own horse. Horses have a way of getting hungry, thirsty, and dirty whether it is a pleasant spring day or raining pitchforks. It is fun to spend time with the horse when the sky is blue. But will you like clomping out to the corral to take care of his needs when the mud is knee deep, and it is cold and rainy?

If your time is well filled with the toils of everyday living and an extra hobby or two, be prepared to let something go. Caring for a horse takes time out of each day. It is a fact that a horse can tie you down. As a horse owner you will not be able to leave town for a few days and tuck the animal in the carport as you could a speedboat. A reliable horse sitter is a must.

Before considering the purchase of a horse, make sure that you can like him. If your reasons for bringing home one of these creatures is to get a little exercise when YOU feel like it, or to add a little prestige to your grounds, forget it. To properly care for a horse, you must sincerely enjoy being with him.

26

Selecting the horse can be a family affair.

If you plan to move into a new area so that you can legally keep a horse or two, check the zoning before buying the property. Consider the type of neighborhood. If, for instance, a new mobile home park or apartment complex has just been erected nearby and most of the remaining neighbors do not have farm animals, be suspicious of a possible zone change within the next few years.

If, after all of these words of caution, you are still determined to own a horse, please read on.

One thing a prospective horse owner should do is to learn all he can about the species. Rent horses and ride often, talk to people who own horses, and read all you can about their care.

The next step is to find the right horse for you. This in itself can be an enjoyable family experience. One popular way in which to locate horses for sale is to read the classified ads in your local newspaper. These ads are usually run by a private party who wants a good home for his horse. One important question to ask these people is: "Why are you selling this horse?" Answers such as, "Because we are moving," "The kids have outgrown their need for him and are advancing to a better horse for show purposes," "Lack of interest as kids are getting older," should cause you to consider the horse further. But comments such as: "He is too much for us to handle," "We just can't keep him in our corral and the neighbors are complaining," "He and my husband don't get along," should cause you to back off.

27

If a certain breed strikes your fancy, seek a breeder of that type of horse. Local feed barns or horse clubs should be helpful in supplying you with information of those in your area.

Trainers have access to information about local horses that are for sale. By informing the trainer of your experience with horses, he can steer you toward the ones that would work best for you.

A horseshoer comes in contact with many horses each week. By chatting with their owners he learns of good buys on horses, too. If it is an animal he has shod several times, he can pass along highlights concerning the animal's temperament.

Feed-store owners rap with numerous horse enthusiasts. Few people will keep it a secret if they have a horse for sale. The bulletin board at the feed barn is a good source of the latest in horses for sale, also.

Horse traders buy and sell horses like used car dealers do cars. Since the trader has many horses, some of them for a very short period of time, he can't really know each of them well. Ask to speak to the previous owner of a horse. You'll find that you'll get more hard truth from people AFTER they have sold their horse.

Most experts suggest that a novice stay away from auctions. They are exciting and interesting to attend, and occasionally one can buy some good tack at an auction. But in the case of horses, what you see is not always what you get.

Many horses are there because they were unable to be sold in a more

The horse should readily accept routine handling.

28

Cute but not practical. Buying a young horse for a child is a dangerous mistake.

conventional way. Think of it, how many loving owners of a gentle, sound, well-mannered horse would take him to an auction to be sold for a small price to someone they've never met?

Try out several horses before making your decision. When I say "try them out," that is exactly what I mean. Observe each horse with an open mind. Watch carefully as the owner works with the horse to ready him for you to ride. Note the animal's reaction to being brushed, bridled, and saddled. Check for lameness as the owner puts him through his paces. But be leery of the horse if his owner won't ride him first.

Notice the condition of his hooves. If they have been grossly neglected, you can bet his health has too.

Insist on being allowed to ride the horse in areas other than his own yard. A small child can ride even a highly spirited horse in a small arena. The real test of how he handles is to take him away from his home.

Ride him more than once. Go back three or four times if necessary, but make sure you can really trust this horse to behave any day, under varied circumstances. The ideal situation is to take the horse home for a two-week trial period before making up your mind. Not all owners will allow this, however.

Make sure this horse can accomplish simple, necessary horse tasks, such as being securely tied without pulling back, moving at a gentle lope without bucking or running away, accepting the bridle without a fuss, lifting his feet without commotion, and trailering well. You may not have a trailer yet, and you may think that you'll never want one, but this manner of conveyance certainly opens up new worlds to you and your horse. Once a horse owner, you will probably eventually want to participate in activities that will take you out of your neighborhood.

Stumbling is another fault to look for. Sometimes this is due to hooves that have been allowed to grow too long or improper shoeing. Sometimes it is a habit that a lazy horse has developed. But it could be a trait that is incurable.

Many people go for the flashy looking, high-headed, ever-moving horse in the beginning. A spirited horse might look impressive as he dances and prances about the premises. It feels exciting to be aboard this flamboyant animal. But a horse of this type will soon become a chore to ride. Eventually, you will lose interest in him.

Stallions are always a poor choice for a young person or a novice rider. With very few exceptions, they are too much for anyone but the most experienced rider to handle.

Mares can be moody. Although many horse owners find them excellent mounts, they can be gentle one day and cranky the next. A mare, however, can be used for breeding if a permanent injury should occur. Geldings are a popular choice for most everyone. They generally have a more even disposition.

A horse under five years of age is very seldom a wise choice for the new rider. Horses are what is considered "settled" after age six or seven. I personally recommend a horse past ten years for a family's first horse. With good care a horse can live into its late twenties.

Don't consider, as some people do with mighty unhappy results, to buy a foal so that he can grow up with your child. Foals have much to learn, and they need proper guidance by an experienced horseperson. They are playful and unpredictable. To expect a child to learn to ride and to train a young horse is asking for too much.

The size of the horse you should buy depends largely on your build.

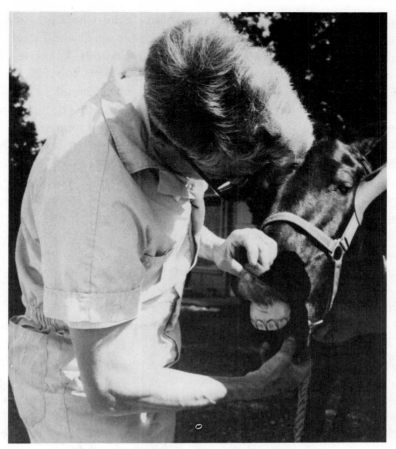

Only a veterinarian will know if the horse is sound.

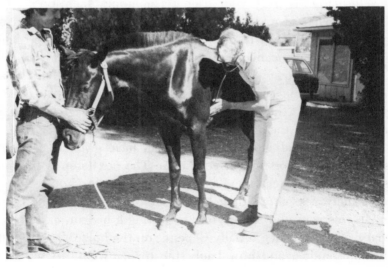

It is best to get a horse that fits you. That is, a pony isn't practical for a man who weighs two hundred pounds. A very small child might have trouble climbing atop a 16-hand horse all by himself. If the animal of your dreams is gentle and safe, even though he is too tall for your youngest daughter to get on by herself, buy him anyway. You'll probably be there whenever she needs a boost. And it is better to have a dependable mount for the family than a proper-sized monster.

While engaging in this fascinating hunt for the perfect horse, it is wise to seek the advice of someone with extensive knowledge of horses, someone who has been around horses for enough years that some horse sense has seeped through his (or her) pores. In most cases this person will be pleased to be able to aid in the purchase of your first horse. A horse lover does not like to see the wrong horse end up under the care of the wrong family. Ask this friend to accompany you on some of your horse-hunting trips. Listen as he questions the owner and pay attention when he explains good and bad points he observes about each horse.

And on that wonderful day when your family has finally agreed on the horse to adopt, be sure that this friend is present to guide you.

Before laying out cash for that horse, spend about thirty dollars and get a vet check. I know that you and your friend have carefully felt each leg, you've probed and poked and cannot see a thing wrong with him. But did you notice if he had wind puffs, splints, arthritis, or ringbone? Does he show signs of stringhalt, sidebones, or ear mites? Of course you didn't notice because you are not a qualified veterinarian. Your veterinarian is truly your friend. The money spent on a vet check will be somewhat of a safeguard against a lame horse or expensive vet bills in the future. He will point out to you the animal's problems, if any, and their significance. For instance, a rope burn or wire cut scar may look unsightly, but for a backyard pleasure horse these blemishes might be of no concern. If the owner refuses to let you have a vet check, don't buy the horse. Some owners will agree to pay the veterinarian's bill if the horse is found to be unsound.

When your friend and the veterinarian have given their respective nods of approval, you are on your own. The next step is the business transaction. Most prices are flexible. As in cars, or houses, the horse owner usually asks more than he intends to get so that he can come down. In this way you think you are getting a bargain and he gets his original price. The price usually depends on the horse's age, bloodlines, condition, training, and how badly the owner wants to sell it. Good grade (unregistered) horses cost anywhere from $100 to $800 depending on where you live. You will soon get an idea of the value of the type of horse you want after seeing plenty of them and comparing prices. Everyone puts a different value on things. The same horse could be sold eight times at eight different prices, depending on the seller's and the buyer's attitude at the time. Just keep in mind that an expensive horse costs the same to keep as a cheaper one.

It is important to obtain a bill of sale. A plain piece of paper with the necessary information written on it will do just fine. A sample bill of sale might read:

> Sold to Marsha Johnston, on May 7th 1973, one sorrel gelding called "Prince." Blaze, 3 socks, brand on left shoulder "S", quarter crack on right fore, age at time of purchase, 10 years.
>
> signed by the sellers

If the horse's bridle is for sale, purchase it if at all possible. If not, see about buying one identical in design. A horse will work better with a bit he is used to.

The next obvious step is to bring your new possession home. If you already have another horse, don't put the new one with the old one until they have had a chance to get acquainted. To accomplish this, you should confine the two horses separately for a few days so that they can see each other but can't touch.

You will no doubt want to ride your new horse right away. It is wise to let him get used to his new surroundings in a calm, uncomplicated atmosphere, however, so don't ask too much of him for the first day or so.

If there are children in the family, strict guidelines are in order. Work closely with them and the horse at first. It takes patience, but the effort is worthwhile. You will be doing something as a family that is enjoyable. You will be teaching the children the right way to behave around the horse, and they will, in turn, develop proper habits. This is important training for these future horsemen and women.

Let the kids ride around the backyard or in another enclosure under your supervision until you feel that they have things pretty well under control. This could take anywhere from a few days to several weeks. Next, walk or ride with them as they amble along the neighborhood paths, making sure they can handle the horse away from his now familiar surroundings.

Lay down your ground rules: no riding double, no running on the pavement, ride only with a saddle, and so on. These dos and don'ts will be made clear in a later chapter.

As soon as possible teach your children to do their own grooming, saddling, and bridling. Stick with them until they have this process mastered.

I realize that you have just brought a half ton of horseflesh home and led it into your corral. You have plans of keeping this horse forever, and maybe you will. But if you do someday decide to sell him to get a different horse or because you are moving, here are some tips.

Write an interesting classified ad. Which of these ads would you answer more readily?

8-year-old bay gelding, make offer. phone no.

or

Gentle bay gelding, perfect for beginners. Sensible on trails and roadways. Asking $250 for this 8-year-old. phone no.

Show consideration and keep appointments with prospective buyers. Show the horse at his best by having him well groomed and his corral clean. He will perform better for the buyer if he is in good condition. This means proper care and consistent exercise.

Since you are used to the horse, it is wise for you to ride him first. He will appear smoother and under better control with a familiar person than with a stranger.

You will be asked many questions about your horse. Answer them truthfully. No matter what your horse is like, there will be someone who will want him, so concentrate on suiting him to the right person.

3 LET'S BE PROPERLY OUTFITTED

Every sport has its own attire. Horseback riding is no different. The main concern here, as in most recreational pastimes, is safety and comfort.

Pants, slightly longer than for normal street wear and of a sturdy, rugged fabric, are best. They should fit snugly, but not so tight that you can't lift your leg to place your foot in the stirrup. We have all seen the romantic picture of the girl who wears shorts as she gallops her horse through a grassy field. No one but she, however, is aware of the irritation she suffers later. Horses sweat. The friction of bare skin against moist horsehair can cause an annoying itch.

Even on warm days it is wise to take along a shirt with long sleeves. That short morning ride could turn into an entire day on the trail. A lightweight shirt could be just enough cover-up to prevent a painful sunburn or an attack by hungry mosquitoes.

If you don't have a cowboy hat yet, buy one. They come in many styles and colors and at a wide range of prices. The hat is not designed to prove to people that you are now a horse owner. It has a much more important purpose. On a damp day the wide brim will keep the moisture off of your head and face, and protect you from the strong sun's rays on a summer day.

A pair of Western boots is a must for anyone who plans to ride in a Western saddle. Even though boots now come in many fancy and plain styles and shades to complement any outfit, they are still designed for your safety. They are sturdy so that if a thousand-pound horse puts his giant hoof on your toe (a surprisingly common occurrence) you have

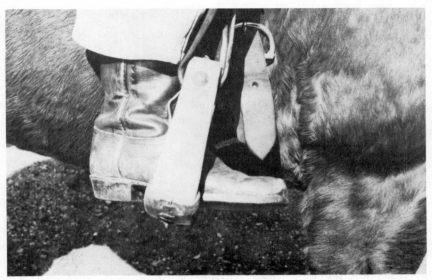

Safety is the main reason for using Western boots with a Western saddle.

some protection. Tennis shoes and sandles have no place around horses.

The Western boot is made to prevent the rider's foot from easily slipping through a stirrup. If, however, a horse were to spook and a boot did get hung up, the foot would simply slip out of it, preventing the rider from being dragged.

Chaps still have the same place in the 1970s as they did in the old West. They provide warmth and protection from thick brush on long trail rides. A more colorful version of the plain old brown leather chaps are the chaps used for the Western classes in horse shows. They may come in any shade, from hot pink to a soft gold. The rider usually coordinates his outfit to go with his chaps. They are fitted to be snug in all areas. The legs are sometimes so tight that it takes two people to get them zipped up. The reason for this is that, in showing, the contestant wants as little extra bulk as possible. A bunch of flopping fabric or leather or a blousy look to his clothes can detract from a smooth, even ride. Many show people decorate their chaps with silver conchos.

For trail riding, a pair of plain brown, loose-fitting, used chaps will do just fine.

Dangling or loopy jewelry has no place around horses. Not only can a nice piece of jewelry be broken, but imagine what would happen if the

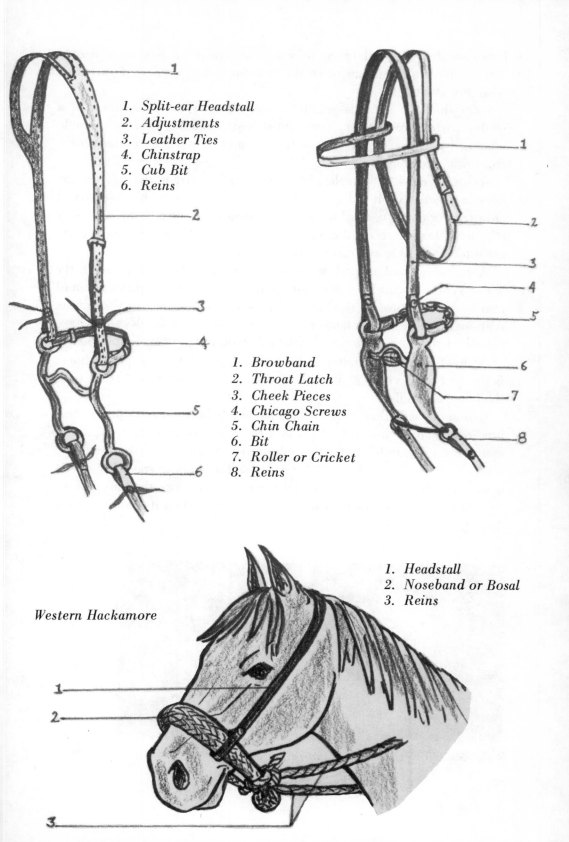

1. Split-ear Headstall
2. Adjustments
3. Leather Ties
4. Chinstrap
5. Cub Bit
6. Reins

1. Browband
2. Throat Latch
3. Cheek Pieces
4. Chicago Screws
5. Chin Chain
6. Bit
7. Roller or Cricket
8. Reins

Western Hackamore

1. Headstall
2. Noseband or Bosal
3. Reins

horse swished his tail catching a coarse strand of hair in a pierced earring. Wear a minimum of small, nonprotruding jewelry, if you must wear any at all.

Now that the rider is set, let's venture into the tack room of a well-outfitted horse. Every horse must have a saddle. There are people who will disagree, but I have seen no good and plenty of bad come from riding bareback.

A bridle consists of a headstall (the leather straps that go on the horse's head), a bit (the metal part that goes into his mouth), a chinstrap (a chain or leather strap that runs under the chin), and reins (the long, leather straps the rider uses to control the horse). These parts are interchangeable and can be bought separately.

A horsehair saddle pad is another necessity. One of those fluffy white synthetic lamb's wool pads that have become so popular could also be used to protect the horse's back from the rubbing of the saddle. Although made with a lamb's wool underside, a saddle does not have sufficient padding for a horse when a 130-pound person climbs aboard.

At least one strong halter and a six- to eight-foot lead rope per horse is the first thing you will need. This is something that is used every time the horse is handled.

Grooming aids that are a must include a rubber curry comb, coarse bristled "dandy" brush, soft bristled finishing brush, hoof pick, and a mane and tail comb. A sturdy rubber bucket can also have many uses around a horse. It can be used for giving water, feed, or special treats. It is also handy for storing your grooming aids because they are always together and can be easily carried to the horse when it is time for his daily grooming session.

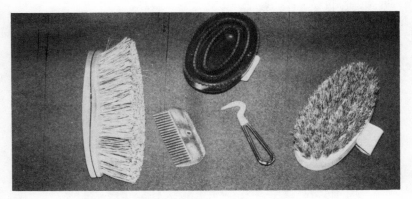

Basic items for grooming the horse.

Before shopping for a horse blanket, measure the horse from the center of the chest to the center of the tail.

Although there are many many more items on the market for the horse owner, those just listed are the ones that every horse owner needs and will most often use.

Here is a list of equipment that is useful, but that isn't necessary for the new horse owner to have immediately. Buy them as you feel you need them.

Another rubber bucket can be handy for traveling or showing. It is wise to provide your own watering vessel when away from home. This minimizes the chances of your horse contracting a communicable disease.

A horse blanket is another optional, and sometimes valuable, item. But before buying one, know why you want it. There are a variety of blankets for a like variety of needs. A day blanket is lightweight and is used to prevent the horse's hair from getting sun bleached while he is out of doors during the day. This type of a blanket is also valuable in keeping a horse clean and the flies away. Trailering a horse is yet another way to use this sheet. The dust will not accumulate on his coat then, and the blanket will protect him from drafts.

A winter blanket is thicker and heavier. This is used on cold winter days and nights to keep the animal from growing a long, shaggy coat. When the days are warm, the blanket is removed each morning and put on each evening. Many people use two blankets at night, and during the slightly warmer daytime, they remove just one of them.

There are also hoods that encompass the horse's entire neck, head, and face. Holes are provided for his ears, eyes, and mouth.

Night blanketing is usually done for show horses. This helps to keep the horse sleek, shining, and looking his very best for the judge.

The only caution here is don't start this blanketing process unless you intend to keep it up. Forgetting to blanket for one chilly night leaves the horse wide open to pnuemonia.

Some blankets are waterproof and make excellent raincoats for horses. Moisture will sometimes soak through during a long, hard rain, and if you can't wait until the rain is over to dry the blanket out, go ahead and remove it periodically while it is raining. Dry it in an automatic dryer and replace it on the horse promptly. He should be kept out of the rain if possible, while waiting for his blanket to dry.

This procedure is recommended for the horse that is used to being blanketed. One that is accustomed to being in the weather should be watched for any signs of chilling, but he will probably need no special treatment.

Most blankets can be washed and dried in the family laundry machines. Check fiber content to be sure.

Blankets are sometimes given as prizes for trail ride competition or shows. These trophies are something to be proud of. We save our "special" blankets for use as trailering sheets, or to cool the horse out at the show. These I call "show off" blankets, and why not show them off?

Many horses don't like to have things flapping around them. They will shy away from someone putting on a jacket in the wind or a line full of blowing laundry. So until the horse gets used to seeing the blanket coming toward him and the feel of it sliding around on his back, use caution in putting it on.

Have the blanket rolled, back to front, inside out. Lay the folded blanket on the horse's withers and unfold it gently toward the back. When it is smooth and straight, fasten the front strap first (across the chest), then the middle one, and the back one last.

In removing the blanket, unfasten the back buckle first, then the middle, and the front one last. Roll the blanket toward the back, keeping the straps from dangling down and touching the legs.

Do not leave an expensive blanket or any other piece of equipment where the horse can get to it. Horses can be as destructive as a bunch of hungry bear cubs.

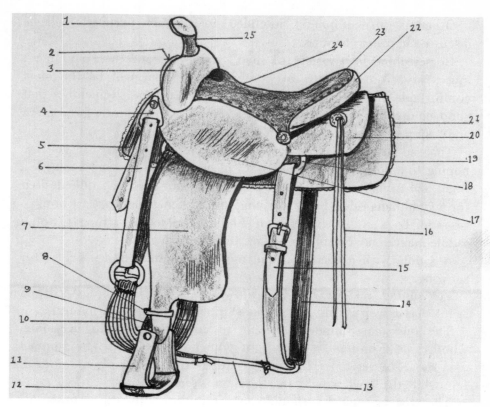

1. Horn Cap	14. Flank Cincha
2. Pommel	15. Flank Billet
3. Fork or Swell	16. Saddle Strings
4. Latigo Holder	17. Seat or Jockey (Side)
5. Front Jockey	18. Dee Ring
6. Latigo	19. Skirt
7. Fender	20. Back Jockey
8. Stirrup Strap	21. Wool Lining
9. Stirrup Leather	22. Cantle Binder
10. Webbed Cinch	23. Cantle Front
11. Stirrup	24. Seat
12. Tread Cover	25. Horn Neck
13. Connector Strap (or Spacer)	

Blankets come in sizes. Measure the horse from the middle of the chest along the side to the middle of the tail. Check the chart at the feed store for the correct size.

Although a pair of old scissors can be used, good horse clippers should eventually be added to a well-equipped tack room.

41

Other useful equipment intended for certain purposes will be discussed in other chapters.

Horses come in a variety of shapes and sizes, and their equipment must vary, too. Be sure to purchase items that will be the most comfortable and serviceable for you and your horse. Remember that good equipment does not depreciate rapidly. If you buy a good piece and take proper care of it, the value will be maintained.

The saddle is the most costly item next to the horse. If you are hoping to indulge in a little riding for pleasure or on the trail, look for a small, lightweight saddle. This would also be the type of saddle desired for a gymkhana rider. For trail riding the leather strings that are used to tie saddlebags and other items on should be intact and strong. If not, a saddle maker may be able to replace them for you.

A saddle with a deep seat and more elaborate in design is best for showing.

For roping, a stout, heavy, shallow-seated saddle is used. A cutting saddle has a deep seat to guard against quick, unplanned dismounts.

The one most important point to consider in buying a saddle, whether used or new, is that it fit your horse and you. The pommel area should never touch the horse's withers and the bars should not rub him while the cinch is tight and the rider is seated.

The rigging (cinch) should not interfere with the horse's leg movement.

Three types of halters are (left to right) nylon rope, flat nylon, and leather.

Saddle seats come in sizes. They range from a 9" seat to an 18" seat. Most saddle shops have a chart to determine the proper seat for you by your weight and height.

An unsuitable or rotten halter invites accidents. There are several types of halters to choose from. Stick to the one that does the best job of containing your horse.

Leather halters cost more and require the most care. They are not strong enough, however, to hold a horse that is tied and that likes to pull back. Leather halters are used for show. They are usually decorated with beautiful silver pieces and come in a wide variety of styles.

A cotton rope halter is practically indestructable. It costs little and is adjustable, but it is not pretty. The trouble with cotton halters is that they will shrink. You must buy the halter large and wet it to shrink it down. If not bone dry when put on a horse, it could tighten up on his face and cause considerable discomfort.

Nylon rope halters last a long time, they stay looking good, and they will not break, or shrink. The price is low on these gems, too.

The newest in halters is the flat nylon webbed ones. They resemble the style of the leather halter. They are more expensive than cotton or nylon, but are easy to keep clean. Although the nylon won't break, the stitching may eventually tear out, causing the halter to come apart. These flat nylon halters fit better under the bridle for trail riding.

The lead rope is important, too. It is recommended that it be a six- to eight-foot length of round rope in a diameter of one-half inch. The flat nylon leads, although attractive, can be dangerous if not properly handled. Even experienced horsepeople have suffered gashes when the horses they were tending pulled the razorlike nylon through their hands.

If you were not able to purchase your horse's bridle with him, you must try to duplicate it now—that is, if it fit well and he worked nicely with it.

Many people make the mistake of making adjustments on a split ear type headstall on just one side. It can cause an awkward fit and an irritation from leather rubbing a tender ear. Make the necessary adjustments on both sides, keeping the ear centered within the enclosure.

When fitting a bit, take into consideration its width and its severity. A dog-gentle horse does not need a severe spade bit. A small pony cannot handle a bit made for a horse.

Most novices have the bit adjustment either too low or too high in the mouth of the horse. Ideally, the corners of the horse's mouth should have slight wrinkles caused by the pressure of the mouthpiece. The wrinkles are sometimes called a "smile." If you will notice, there is one area in the horse's mouth where he has no teeth. The bit should fit into this space.

The chinstrap helps greatly to control the horse, and it should also fit properly. When adjusted correctly, one or two fingers will fit between the strap and the horse's chin when the reins are relaxed. With your fingers there, pull back on the reins and feel the pressure. This is a good demonstration to give a child who is forever yanking on the horse's reins. Show him how it feels.

When the chinstrap is too loose, it has no real purpose except to occasionally pinch the skin around the horse's mouth. A chinstrap that is too tight can cause undue discomfort, too.

You can buy tack at many of the same places where horses are sold. Watch want ads in the paper and bulletin boards around town. Most saddle shops carry new and used tack. Auctions are good places to buy tack. Get there in plenty of time so that you can examine the merchandise prior to the sale. Know what tack is selling for and be ready with your highest bid. Don't get swept up into the excitement and overbid. Know what items you need and bid only on those.

It is imperative to the longevity of the equipment that it is properly cared for. Carefully tended to, it can outlast several horses.

These portable racks are an excellent way to store saddles.

This is the correct way to "rest" a saddle when a rack is not immediately available.

There are right and wrong ways of storing equipment. Whether it be a heated and air-conditioned tack room with its own swimming pool or a cleared-out corner of a garage, you can take certain precautions.

A one-pound coffee can nailed to the wall makes a good place to hang a bridle and a halter. Using a nail for this purpose causes a greater degree and concentration of pressure at one point on the bridle, and the leather can begin to wear in that spot.

The saddle must be stored off the ground, as with the bridle. Hang a saddle from the rafters by the horn and pommel. Make simple wooden saddle racks that protrude from the wall, use an old sawhorse, or get fancy and design interesting and unique saddle caddies of your own.

Never lay the saddle flat on the ground or on the leather seat. Keep the lamb's wool padding out of stickers and dirt. To set the saddle down temporarily, balance it on the horn and pommel and lay blankets and pad, sweaty side up, over the saddle.

When bridling a horse, never allow the reins to drag on the ground. Hold them up away from the horse's feet at all times. Horses have a way of moving around at the wrong time, and many sets of reins have been broken by disregarding this warning.

If a piece of equipment does not fit the horse just right, make it fit. If the stirrups can't be adjusted to the most comfortable position for the rider by using the available holes, punch new ones; and do it now. If you don't have a leather punch, borrow one and make everything so that it fits right.

When stirrup holes become elongated, as they will on the left side from stress of constant mounting and dismounting, tie a strip of rawhide through the holes to help fill the gap.

Never, never tie a horse with the reins. All beginner horse books make this statement, and yet you still see people carelessly tying their horses with the reins. There are several reasons for heeding this warning of mine and of every knowledgeable horseperson. First, if the horse should try to break away because he became startled or bored, he could cut his mouth with the bit. Also, if he should rub his head on the hitching post or even his own leg, he could very easily rub his bridle right off of his head and he would be loose. Thirdly, as I mentioned before, leather halters are not made sturdy enough to hold a horse, and neither are leather bridles. Reins break very easily when a horse is applying strength to them. Equipment is costly. Protect your investment in your tack and your horse, be cautious, and use common sense.

Never wrap the reins or lead rope around hands, arm, waist, or any other part of you. Fold excess leather or rope flat in your hand. There's no possible way a man can hold a horse that is bent on escaping. No matter how good of a grip a man has on the animal, the horse always has a stronger one.

Don't hook the lead rope to the bit for tying or leading purposes. This practice could cause damage to his mouth.

Check the cinch, latigo straps, Chicago screws, and other points of pressure, wear, and friction periodically. A major cause of horse accidents is faulty equipment. Don't take chances, give it a thorough going over, and repair or replace any old or frayed parts.

Can you imagine what happens when the copper part of the mouthpiece of the bit comes loose and the sharp edges poke the horse's mouth each time you pull the reins?

There have been countless accidents, some quite serious, when a stirrup has come off while riding, or a latigo strap has broken. Even the

46

Checking your equipment often for wear could prevent a disaster while riding.

breaking of a smaller strip of leather such as the spacer that runs between the front and back cinch, or the chin strap, can cause a confused reaction by the horse when the strap flops and slaps him unexpectedly. A rein breaking during a full-out run across a meadow can be a dangerous situation. So check this equipment before getting on the horse. Give it a test for stress before the horse does. Better the faulty leather comes apart in your hand than while riding far from home.

Keeping tack clean will make it last longer. Many people don't realize that every piece of equipment should be washed.

The horsehair pads can be hosed off and scrubbed with mild suds. Use a rubber curry or stiff brush to get out the accumulated dirt. Then spray with clean water until all of the soap is removed. Slide the edges

Your saddle will last longer if taken care of properly.

of your hands across the pad sharply to draw out the excess water and hang the damp pad over a fence to dry.

To keep the leather clean between saddle soapings, wipe the saddle and bridle with a rag after each ride.

Brush the lamb's wool padding with a stiff brush to remove any foreign material and spray it with moth repellent once a year.

Every few months wash the saddle with Castile soap and water. Be sure to scrub all parts. With an almost dry sponge, apply saddle soap. Rub a generous amount of the soap into the leather and let it dry thoroughly. Next rub vigorously with a soft, dry cloth. This will cause a sheen and will help to fill the pores and scrapes on the surfaces of the leather.

To replenish natural oils in parts that come in constant contact with the horse, use Neatsfoot oil.

An old toothbrush is useful to clean the bit and other metal pieces. Wash metal with soap and water. Apply metal or silver polish to remove stains and tarnish. Then wipe all polish from the bit.

Mice love to nibble on leather, so it is important to keep it out of their reach. Dampness is another enemy. Store the saddles and bridles in a dry place and wipe them down after each use.

4 GROOMING AND THE HEALTHY HORSE

There are many important reasons for grooming a horse regularly. It helps to "gentle" a horse. A well-groomed horse has a healthier coat because the skin is stimulated and natural oils give the hair a sheen. His circulation is improved by the messaging effects of brushing. It also promotes a good muscle tone. A horse that is groomed often is easier to keep clean for those special occasions. Any skin problems that spring up are noticed immediately when such constant care is a habit, and treatment can begin before the disease gets out of hand.

Not only does the horse benefit greatly from this daily grooming, but so does his owner. The time you spend grooming your horse can be the most enjoyable minutes of the day— just you and him getting to know each other better.

Grooming should take place every day of the year. But during spring, horse owners have a few months of heavy grooming ahead of them. They must begin to help the horse's winter growth of hair to shed.

Always groom a horse thoroughly before riding. A sloppy job of brushing can leave enough dirt to cause him the pain of saddle sores. A burr left hidden in a thick coat could do even more damage.

It feels good to a horse to have the irritating sweat wiped away from his face and saddle area with a cool damp sponge after each ride.

The first step in grooming a horse is to catch him. If he is in a stall or other small enclosure, make sure he knows of your presence as you enter. Use a low, comforting voice tone as you approach. Make the horse face you. An unaware horse could (and very often does) kick out when he is suddenly startled.

50

Tara Stebbins and her horse both enjoy this essential part of horse grooming.

Springtime means natural shedding of the horse's winter coat. A shedding blade helps.

It is sometimes more difficult to get near the horse that is kept in a large area, but each horse is different. Some love people and will run up to them with no encouragement. Others prolong the inevitable of being caught as long as possible. For those horses who do not know that word "cooperation," a bucket of grain sometimes helps. It rarely does, however, if it is used ONLY when the horse is to be ridden. It is a good idea to catch the horse often just to feed him a treat so that he does not associate feed with work.

If there is more than one horse in the pasture, sometimes it is necessary to catch and tie the others. A horse is always easier to catch when alone. This may sound silly, I mean if you can't catch the horse that you want, how are you going to catch the other horses? Well, it is surprising how the pastured horses seem to know which horse you are after, and they sometimes will do everything within their power to keep you from completing the task. You will find that all of the horses will be easy to catch except the one that you want.

A horse can spot a person who wants to ride by the halter that dangles from his hand, so camouflage it as best you can.

If the horse won't come to you, even for his feed, walk toward him slowly. Never chase him unless you think you can outrun a horse. If he moves away from you, try to edge him into a corner. Many pastures contain a "catch pen." This is a small enclosure within the larger one. It is usually constructed in a corner of the pasture and has its own gate. It is simple to build. The gate is left open and out of the way so that the horses are used to being in this area without the trauma of getting caught each time. If the pursued horse can be cornered into this enclosure and the gate can be closed before he escapes, he is caught.

There is the occasional outlaw animal who would just as soon run you down as to eat from your feed bucket, but these horses are in the minority.

Once you are near enough, slip your arms slowly, but with conviction, around his neck. Next slide the lead rope around his neck to hold him more securely while you put the halter on. To put the halter on, bring it up from under his chin. Slip it onto his nose, pulling the two open ends up (one in each hand) and behind the ears. Quickly fasten it.

All movements should be slow and quiet, but precise. Once caught, let your horse eat a little and pet him and tell him what a good boy he is.

Lead the horse to the grooming area. You will need an open area that is flat and where there are no obstacles to endanger him should he become restless.

Tie him to a solid object. A ladder that is leaning against the barn, a tack room door, a swing set, or a partially rotted fence rail are NOT solid objects. Always, before tying a horse, consider what would happen if the horse got frightened and pulled back. Would the object hold up under the yank of a thousand-pound horse? Consider it seriously, because it does happen. Even the gentlest, most sensible horses can be startled by the unexpected sight of a cat leaping from the tack room roof above him. A sudden gust of wind could bring with it an alarming section of air-born newspaper.

Just imagine the damage a startled horse could to just to himself while running scared, at full speed with a large tree limb, ladder, or splintered fence post bouncing after him. I once saw a horse pull a four-foot-tall decorative yard light onto a busy highway.

Tie the horse so that there are two feet of rope between his halter and the object. His head should be high enough so that he can't get a leg over the rope and low enough so that he is comfortable.

Now then, with the rubber curry comb, use circular motions to loosen deep-down and caked-on dirt from the entire body. Do not use it on the boney areas such as the face and lower legs (below hocks and knees). A damp sponge will aid in removing dried mud from these areas.

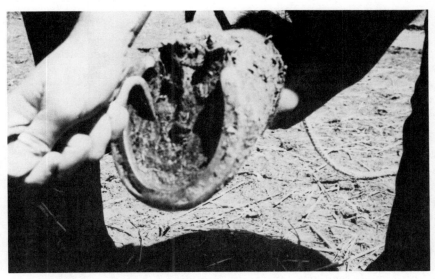

This is the proper way to clean a hoof.

Next, use the stiff brush. With quick, strong, flicking motions, brush the body hair with its normal growth. Start at the neck, chest, and withers. Then move to the shoulder and continue down the foreleg to the knee. Brush the backside in the same manner. Then move along to the belly, rump, and hindleg to the hock. While moving around the horse, keep one hand on him so that he will know where you are at all times. This is important to remember, because a horse's area of vision is limited.

The softer brush can now be used on the face, lower legs, and to pick up loosened dust particles on the body coat. Comb tangles from the mane and tail using the comb. Start at the bottom and work up until all of the hairs are separated. Wipe ears, face, eyes, nostrils, lips, sheath, and dock with a grooming cloth or damp sponge. A gentle wiping on these more tender areas will suffice.

The hooves need to be cleaned before and after each ride and at each grooming session. To clean the left fore hoof, stand close to the horse at his left shoulder facing to the rear. Put your left hand on his shoulder and run it down his leg. As you bend down to grasp the hoof, nudge his shoulder with yours to change his weight distribution so that you may more easily lift the hoof. Secure a good grip on the handle of the hoof pick. With the point aimed away from you, dig all foreign matter from hoof. Always clean hooves from the heel toward the toe.

Most horses wear shoes. Yours, too, will need them if he is ridden regularly, if you ride in rocky areas, if you trail ride often, if the hooves

Your horse needs regular attention by a qualified farrier.

split and crack easily, or if the horse is particularly tender footed. Ponies have tough feet and usually don't require shoeing. Every horsey town will have at least one farrier. Find the name of a good one, and plan to have him come to either reset or change the shoes on your horse every six to eight weeks. A pony or horse that does not wear shoes also needs consistent hoof care. Every six to ten weeks the hooves should be trimmed professionally.

Just as with dogs and cats, horses, too, have preferences in people. If your farrier, for instance, has trouble shoeing your horse because he doesn't want to cooperate with the man, perhaps the answer is a different shoer. This does not mean that the shoer is incompetent. It is just that a person with a different sort of personality might be able to complete the job with much less trouble. I have seen this to be true too many times to pass up mentioning it.

Sometimes a simple solution to the problem of an unmannerly horse at shoeing time is for the owner to make him (or her) self scarce.

A bridle path is both attractive and practical.

This ideal bath rack is not complicated to construct and could fit easily in any backyard.

The hair (feathers) that grow long at the fetlocks can be trimmed with scissors or horse clippers every six months or so. This prevents burrs from accumulating in this area. Be careful not to cut the piece of horny material that protrudes there.

A bridle path affords a place to strap the halter and bridle without the problem of catching or tangling the mane hair. Using scissors or clippers, cut the mane to the skin from pole (or top of the head) to about three to six inches back. Repeat this as necessary.

A bath is usually in order if the horse is going to participate in a parade or compete in a show or if he is just very dirty. Choose a warm day. Plan to give the bath early in the day. Good places for a bath are a flat dirt, blacktop, cement, or grassy area. Grass is best, especially for a fidgety horse who might fall on the more slippery surfaces.

Do not use a noisey spray nozzle on the hose. Turn the water on slowly. Run the water on his lower legs first. Slowly work it up to his back, soaking all but his head.

Using horse shampoo or a mild human brand mixed with warm water, scrub the horse's body with a plastic washing brush.

Don't dawdle. Finish each step quickly so that the horse does not become restless and so that he isn't wet for too long.

Thoroughly rinse the suds off with the hose. A diluted cream rinse

This horse will look neater after his fetlock is trimmed, and he will not be troubled with burrs.

can be used on the mane and tail. This helps eliminate static electricity and makes the tail and mane easier to comb. Then using a sweat scraper, squeeze the excess water out of his coat. Wash his face and ears with a damp cloth.

Next, rub him down with dry, fluffy beach towels.

Walk him or let him stand in the sun until dry. Don't put him away wet.

He'll probably roll as soon as you put him away, and it may be necessary to cover him with a day sheet to help keep him clean overnight.

During the summer months, when flies are at their worst, an item that should be included in a well-stocked tack room is a good fly repellent. The aerosol type is very handy, but some horses shy from the sound the spray makes. Most people use fly wipe. If you keep the rag or sponge that is used with the fly wipe in a coffee can with a plastic lid, they will always be moist because the repellent won't evaporate as quickly. Use the wipe or spray every day for the comfort of your horse.

Grooming tools should be kept clean. Tap the currycomb on your boot to knock the dirt off. Brushes can be cleaned out with the teeth of the currycomb. A soap-and-water soak won't hurt this equipment from time to time.

As you spend more and more time with your horse on the trail, on neighborhood pathways, in the arena, or at the stable, you will grow to know him. You'll learn what his normal behavior and habits are. Because of this you will be the first to notice if something is wrong. You are the best judge as to whether he is well or ill.

Call a veterinarian at the first sign of illness. That means if his temperature is above 102, if he is lame, if he slobbers and seems to be having trouble eating, or if he is off his feed completely. If there is a yellowish discharge from the nose, signs of bleeding anywhere, or if he keeps getting up and down and rolling, call a veterinarian.

Make notes of his behavior pattern while waiting for the veterinarian to arrive.

Some of the common ailments to hit backyard stables are:

1. Colic. Sudden changes in feed, working too soon after eating, errors in feeding, eating while fatigued, drinking in excess while overheated, overindulging in too rich of feed, and parasites such as blood worms are all causes of colic.

Symptoms of this uncomfortable illness are pawing the ground, stretching the body out, continuously turning the head toward the side,

When colic is suspected, the horse should be encouraged to keep walking and not be allowed to roll.

getting up and down, rolling over and over again, groaning, and kicking at the abdomen.

Colic in horses is the equivalent of a bad stomach ache in a human. The problem here is that a horse has no way of vomiting; he can't expell the problems.

Quick treatment is imperative with a colicky horse. Begin walking him immediately; call your veterinarian. Colic can be, and often is, fatal.

2. Colds. Horses usually get colds from other sick horses, or by drinking after infected horses from community watering troughs.

The symptoms include runny nose and eyes, coughing, and going off feed. To treat a cold, let the horse rest. A cold can go into pneumonia if the horse is worked while he is ill. As usual, call a veterinarian.

3. Fever. A horse standing around with his head down for a long period of time could have a fever.

Keep this horse warm and dry. If he has no shelter from the weather on a damp day, use the garage. A blanket will help to keep him warm. Take his temperature by sliding the bulb end of a rectal thermometer into the anus about two inches. Leave it in place for two minutes. A normal temperature for a horse is 99 to 101.

The normal pulse rate for an adult horse that is resting is 36 to 57 beats per minute. Respiration rate is 12 to 13 per minute.

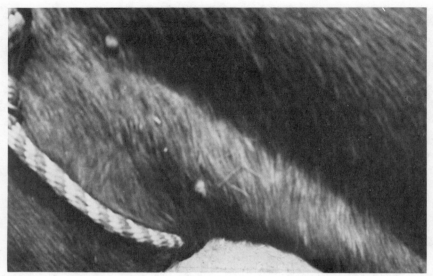

When bringing your horse in from pasture or a trail ride, check for ticks.

4. Injury. Almost every horse owner will have a wound to treat at one time or another. Horses seem to acquire cuts, scrapes, gashes, punctures, and lacerations more easily than any other animal.

Many a horse past the age of nine or ten carry with them scars in the form of thin black lines around the chest and lower legs, indicating that they had an argument with a wire fence and lost.

A large or small wound should be kept clean and free of germ-carrying flies. Do not use an antiseptic, which will cause the wound to become dry or which will further injure the tender tissue. Man cannot heal, only nature can. So to avoid interfering with the healing process, use a good, mild wound dressing that will keep the wound moist and help it to heal naturally.

If the horse is bleeding profusely, stop the flow of blood by applying pressure to the wound.

Keep the horse still. Cover the wound with clean pieces of sheet to keep the dirt and flies off of it. If the injury is to the shoulder or body, drape a sheet over it. The veterinarian should be called if the wound is particularly deep, wide, or if bleeding is uncontrollable or if infection should set in.

Prevention is the best way to approach illness or injury. Although a recommended health program varies slightly from area to area, the main

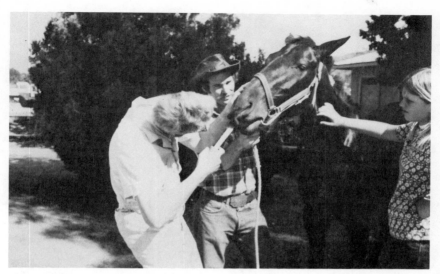

This horse is only four years old and already needs his teeth floated.

vaccination requirements are: tetenus, sleeping sickness (equine encephalomyelitis), influenza, and distemper.

The veterinarian is also a horse dentist. Yes, even horses need their teeth checked for more than just their age. Molars sometimes develop jagged edges that can cut into the horse's mouth or tongue and cause considerable irritation while he is eating. This problem is particularly prevalent in horses under six and those over thirteen years of age. A horse who has suddenly lost weight, or who isn't putting any on, one who is dribbling food from his mouth as he eats, may be in need of having his teeth "floated." The veterinarian, using a special rasp, will file the teeth down so that the horse may again eat in comfort.

Parasites are another major problem in the backyard, pastured, stabled, or pampered horse. Parasites can drastically interfere with the horse's growth, development, and performance. Not only that, but an infested horse loses his resistance to disease.

A foal needs to be wormed by a veterinarian every eight weeks. A grown horse requires the treatment twice a year, every year.

To help prevent parasites, keep the horse's living quarters clean and free of manure.

Ideally, horses should have a clean supply of water available at all times—except after heavy work. Keep in mind that an average horse will drink approximately ten gallons of water a day.

Salt should also be available.

61

5 WHERE SHALL WE KEEP HIM AND
WHAT SHALL WE FEED HIM?

Most parents, when their child asks, "Why won't you buy me a horse?," will say, "We have no place to keep one." This may seem like a put-off to the child, but a proper home for the creature is important.

The ideal place, of course, is in your own backyard. If this is impossible because of zoning laws, cranky neighbors, or lack of restraint to keep him safe, then his home may have to be away from yours.

You will have more contact with your horse if he lives close to you. The farther away he is, the more time it will take to get to him, and soon your interest in riding could begin to diminish.

Sometimes a horse owner is lucky enough to find someone who will board his horse for free. Perhaps someone in their family loves to ride, and the horse could be shared as payment for board. A trade might be feasible in some cases. Think about it. Do you have a service that you could offer in trade? If they have children, perhaps your part of the bargain could be baby-sitting or housework. An older couple may enjoy boarding your horse in exchange for you keeping up their yard.

There are persons who board horses as a business. Contact the ones near you. Ask what services they offer and the price they charge for each. Consider only those services which you will need. Training, riding lessons, stalls, and small pastures that will hold up to three or more horses are often some of the choices available. The price may differ, depending on whether you feed or they do. Be sure to consider your

It is important to keep an eye on the condition of the horse and the pasture.

Remove potentially harmful objects from corral or pasture before allowing the horse to enter.

time and gas in making the decisions. It may not be worthwhile for you to do the feeding if you have to go many miles out of your way.

A pasture is much cheaper than a stable, for there is no need to provide hay for at least part of the year. How much of the year depends on the size of the area, quality of the feed, and number of horses using the pasture. On the negative side, your horse might be harder to catch if he is in a large area with other horses.

63

This is one type of wooden corral. Make sure you have rails on inside of posts.

If your horse is to be kept in a pasture, you will not be required to exercise him as often as the horse that is kept in a small space. Don't ignore him completely, though. It is important to keep a close eye on the condition of the horse and grazing land.

Before placing a horse in a pasture, walk the whole area and check for potentially dangerous objects. Remove all debris, glass, tin cans, boards, and wire, and fill in any large holes. Repair bad places in the fence. Check the water supply and find out who is responsible for it.

Don't turn your horse loose with other horses. Stay around and make sure that the animals have a friendly attitude toward one another. A friend of ours neglected to take the time to see that his pony was going to be accepted by four horses in a pasture. After he dropped the pony off, he left. The larger horses resented the pony's presence and began picking on him. They finally managed to break one of his legs. He had to be destroyed that same day.

Don't, under any circumstances, leave a halter on a horse in a pasture. Not only are there trees, fence posts, and such that he could get hung up on, but there have been incidents where a horse, while rolling, has caught a hoof in a halter. The result is often fatal.

If you have proper zoning and the room on your property, you will more than likely want to build your own facility.

This is a pipe corral.

This corral is constructed of pipe and cable.

Let's start where most horse owners start—with a corral. Wood seems to be most widely used. In building this wooden enclosure for your horse, remember that he is heavy and strong. The posts and rails have got to stand up under 1,200 pounds of leaning, pushing horseflesh. There must not be sharp edges, protruding nails, or hardware that he can tear himself on, because he will, if there is. The rails go on the inside of the posts. I once knew a man who nailed all of his fence rails to the outside of the posts. He wanted the structure to be attractive from the outside. He couldn't understand why, when his horse would lean on the enclosure, the rails would pop off and the horse would escape. The man finally discovered his mistake and reconstructed the corral before a tragedy occurred.

The rails should not be too far apart, or too high off the ground. Even if your horse is not a known escape artist, the corral might someday house one that is.

An average size for a corral is 10' to 12'.

Wood corrals are not for everyone. Some horses like to eat them as fast as their owners can replace the rails. To prevent this annoying habit some people nail a metal stripping across the top of the rails. It is usually a bored horse who chews wood. Building a corral, although not a major construction job, is work. You might as well think ahead so that you, or someone else, won't have to spend many hours repairing it.

A horse likes to see what is going on around him, so don't confine him behind a solid fence.

A pipe corral has always been our favorite way of keeping the horses confined. They can't chew the pipe rails as they can wood. There are no splinters or nails that can work loose and cause a hazard for the horse. Even the most persistent horse can't break down a sturdy pipe corral.

Portable corrals are made of smaller pipe. They can be purchased with or without shelters, feed bins, and watering devices. These lightweight corrals can be set up anywhere. This enables a person to take his corral with him when he moves. Sometimes a person will set up a portable corral in an open pasture. When the grass is all consumed within the corral, it can be moved to another area in the field.

Some people run steel cable through holes in wood or pipe posts to make a safe and sturdy corral.

Many horse enclosures are constructed of wire. This can be satisfactory for the roomy pasture, but not for a small, backyard corral. Barbed wire is the worst possible material to use around horses. A horse is forever rubbing, nudging, pawing, and otherwise coming in contact with his surroundings. The danger of him getting cut on the barbed pieces of the wire is great. Smooth wire is not suitable either. As with barbed wire or chain-link fencing, he can catch a shoe on it. He can push it out of shape, causing an easy escape for him and an unsightly facility for you.

Horses are not stupid. A smart one can cause the greatest amount of trouble. You have to outthink the horse when you make your choice of the type of latch on your corral gate. Ordinary gate latches are for ordinary horses, and even some of them can manage to open these

This is a perfect facility for horses and their care.

fasteners. The majority of the corrals I have seen have rope tied around the gate to reinforce the original latch. This indicates to me that the horses have learned to outsmart their owners.

Horses have gone for years and years without any shelter except for the trees that have dotted their wilderness. You will notice that during a rain storm, the pastured horse lowers his head and faces away from the direction of the rain. This allows his rear end to take the brunt of the storm.

Most backyard horses however are accustomed to the luxury of a proper shelter. The horse needs and will always use available shade on a hot day, be it a tree, lean-to shelter, or a complete barn facility. But even when provided with a place out of the bad weather, he may not use it.

As a horse owner you will not only need a place to keep at least one horse, but you'll have to have a place to store hay and tack. For some, a barn is the answer. A barn might include two enclosed stalls, a room for hay and tack, and a place to work with the horse when the weather is extreme. By that I mean to groom him or to administer medication.

There should be windows in an enclosed stall. Windows should be high enough to prevent a draft and still provide air circulation for the comfort of the horse. A horse that is constantly closed behind four walls will become bored. This can cause him to become cranky and unruly when you want to ride. Windows that can be closed at night are often the answer.

Try to plan your barn so that your horse will have a view that envelopes more than a block wall, a hedge, or the side of a hill. He might like to see children at play, other horses, or cattle; even a dog will help keep him company. Remember, the more confined the horse, the more exercise he'll need. This is not only important for his physical health but also for his mental well-being.

Most barns are built with electrical outlets for lights and so that the electric clippers can be used. Be extremely careful where these outlets and wires are placed. Put them out of the horse's reach. Recess the light bulbs into the ceiling and cover them with a heavy wire mesh.

I knew a man who lost a good colt when the little guy became bored, standing day after day in a soggy corral during a week-long rainstorm. He reached up and grabbed a live electrical wire that dangled from a row of lights over his corral, with his teeth. The result was instant electrocution.

Faucets are also a fascination to a bored or playful horse. Do not place them inside the stall area. Make sure that all plumbing is where the horse isn't likely to stumble over it or play with it.

Is a complete barn too elaborate for a backyard rider such as you? Consider, then, another satisfactory way of storing your tack. Remember that convenience is important. The closer the tack and the horse are together, the better. You are less likely to lose tack if it is not a hassle to put it away after each use.

If you cannot build a small place to keep tack, consider buying a used building that could be hauled in for that purpose. One of those aluminum garden tool storage sheds is what many backyard and professional horsemen use.

A corner of the garage is always a satisfactory place, too.

Tack is easy to resell. There are people who steal horse equipment and sell it for a small price. If your tack room or garage has a lock on it, use it. If not, you may want to keep the more valuable pieces of tack in the house.

Keep the horse's living quarters clean. Fifteen minutes of cleaning a day will pretty much assure you of sanitary grounds. There are people who use horse manure in their gardens. By advertising that you have manure, you may find someone who will take it off your hands, thus minimizing your responsibility.

To feed a horse off the ground is to invite problems. He can pick up

This is an oil barrel feed bin.

parasites this way. The dirt he gets with his feed might cause him major intestinal damage. The practice of ground feeding also wastes hay.

There are many types of feed bins for use in stalls or corrals. Feed and tack stores sell feeders. If you prefer not to buy one, check various designs and consider constructing one at home. Remember, don't leave sharp edges.

A wooden feeder.

The perfect manger height for a full-sized horse is 38" to 42" off the ground. The manger should slope up from where it is nailed to the wall to protect his knees. It is best to have the feed bin secured in some manner. Lightweight metal feed pails that are not secured get terribly dented as the horse kicks them around.

Some people use fifty-five-gallon metal drums to feed from. There are many ways in which they can be installed as feeders. Be sure to roll all cut edges so that there are no sharp places. Or use the barrel as is. Simply fill the bottom with rocks or bricks so it can't be knocked over and he can reach the feed.

Rubber tires are used sometimes as feeders. Some horses, however, will eat the rubber. This can cause serious intestinal distress.

You'll find that three-quarters of the amount of the entire cost of a horse's needs is feed. Hay is the bulk of his diet.

The types of hay vary with the area. The most economical way to purchase hay is by the ton during the summer or fall.

It is wise to try a few bales before buying in quantity. Break it open and examine it thoroughly. If it seems to be good hay, full of oats, grain, or leaves (depending on the type of hay), if it is free of mold and does not smell musty, go ahead and feed.

If you have accidentally acquired some bad hay, do not keep it on the property. A horse could get out and eat it, or someone might feed it to him.

By buying hay directly from the farmer and hauling it yourself, you will make another savings. Use your pick-up, horse trailer, or utility trailer, or rent one of these useful vehicals. If you pay for the feed, the farmer might store it for you if you aren't able to take it all then.

If you haven't proper storage for the hay, you could lose it to mold. Moldy hay will kill a horse.

Store hay off of the ground on wooden slats or pallets and cover with waterproof tarps in damp weather, if inside storage is not available. Sometimes it pays to store the hay in a dry garage and leave the family car out.

Alfalfa pellets are easier to store, and they have many added nutrients. There is less waste, and pellets are less messy to feed.

Keep feed behind locked doors if at all possible. A horse could get out and find the grain bag, causing himself permanent damage or even death.

When feeding several horses in a large corral where there are not enough feed bins, give them separate rations. Make as many piles as there are horses. Put the piles far enough apart that the horses won't get into a kicking fight. If you have one horse that gets grain, use a feed bag so that he will be the only one getting it.

Horses vary in their capacity for consuming food just as humans do. An "easy keeper" is the term given the horse that seems to stay fat or

One sure way of choosing the right amount of feed is to weigh it.

71

Hold hand open to avoid getting bitten while feeding treats.

even gain weight on a minimum of feed. Then there are the horses that require much more food to maintain a normal weight.

Following is a suggested feeding schedule for a horse of good health and who is free of worms. (This average horse weighs 1,000 pounds.) An idle horse should consume fourteen pounds of hay a day, and there is no need for grain. A horse that does light work, say around two hours a day, can be fed fourteen pounds of hay and four pounds of grain a day. A horse that works four hours a day or so can eat fifteen pounds of hay and five pounds of grain. A horse that puts in a long seven-hour day will find fifteen pounds of hay and ten pounds of grain the right amount of feed for him. Breeding animals and young horses require a different schedule.

Observe the weight gain or loss and the general appearance of your horse and adjust this feeding schedule accordingly.

To determine the weight of your horse there are weight tapes for sale at feed stores. Measure around the girth. The tape is usually right within fifty pounds.

If a change in feed is necessary, do it gradually and carefully. Introduce new feed in small rations with regular feed. Increase the new feed each day until the switch is made.

Feed twice daily at approximately the same time each day. This is most important for the digestion of the horse, and consequently his health.

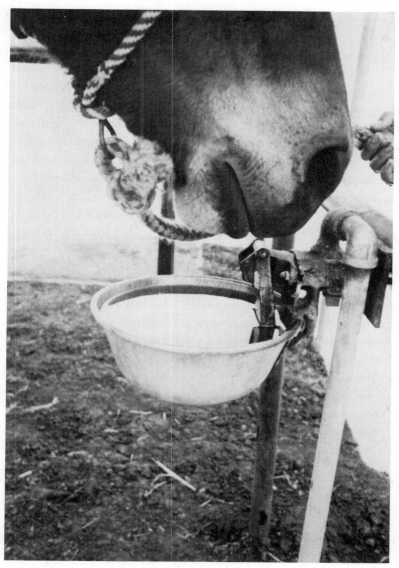

An excellent watering device is the automatic waterer.

Many of us love to give our horses special treats. It helps in catching a horse that wants to play hide and seek games and is a way of rewarding a horse for a job well done. We don't know if he gets as much satisfaction from this practice as his Homo sapien friends, but sometimes it seems so.

Our daughter, Penny, used to fix her Appaloosa mare, Peaches, a birthday treat each year. She spent hours mixing the various household oats, cereals, and other grains with chopped carrots, apples, and a dash of brown sugar. She would top it off with Peaches's favorite fruit, strawberries.

There are problems that can result from feeding these special tidbits. A horse could begin the habit of nibbling. If not properly presented with open palm of the hand, the treat might include a finger or two. It is best (for these reasons) to feed treats in small pieces from a bucket.

Some treats that horses like are the commercial horse treats, or fresh carrots, apples, pears, and carrot tops. Other horses have been known to go bananas over watermelon, oranges, tuna sandwiches, cola, and mai tais. Use caution in feeding this sort of junk to horses. Too much can make him sick. A little is a treat and that is what you are trying to give him.

Cool, clean water should be available at all times. A horse can never get too much water. The only exception to this rule is when he is overheated. If the horse is to continue to work at a strenuous pace, the water shouldn't hurt him, but when he is cooling off after a hard work day, water should be given in very small amounts until he is completely cool.

The automatic watering device for corral, stall, or pasture is the ideal way to offer fresh water at all times. Stay around to make sure that your horse can operate the mechanism. Bathtubs can be purchased at small cost from plumbing shops. These are popular because they hold a large supply of water and are heavy enough that they don't get knocked over.

A rubber bucket can be used, but it is best to keep it suspended by a snap off of the floor, so that the horse doesn't continuously knock it over. The bucket will need to be filled three or four times a day.

The block form of salt is preferred. To keep the block from getting lost among the manure and spilled hay, buy a specially designed rack to hold it. This will fasten to the wall or fence and the horse can always find it.

6 THE ETIQUETTE AND HORSE SENSE OF RIDING

Now that you have your horse and you know what to feed him, how to groom him, where to keep him, and the proper riding attire, let's ready him for what you bought him for, to ride.

He is your horse. You can ride any time and for as long as you want. You needn't pay someone for a one-hour ride on a stable horse. You don't have to take turns with a friend on his horse. You can ride at dawn and watch the countryside awaken from its gray sleep into a brilliance of color. You and your horse can enjoy the last glow of sunshine. You can hear the bird's ending melody of the day and the first cricket songs of the evening while riding at dusk. Together, you can get to know even another dimension of riding, the moonlight ride.

The only time you shouldn't ride a well and sound horse is after he has just eaten a big meal. A strenuous ride after a full ration of hay is as bad for him as a full set of tennis is for you after a Thanksgiving feast.

With the grooming done, you are now ready to saddle your mount. First, lay the saddle pad, hair side down, well up on the withers. Then drag it back five or six inches to stroke the hairs back in the direction that they grow. The pad should cover the withers slightly and should be balanced on the back. There should be no wrinkles in the pad.

Use a wool saddle blanket to cover the pad if you wish. They are colorful and look more attractive than the plain horsehair pad.

Pull the cinch and right stirrup over the seat of the saddle, and from the left side of the horse, ease the saddle onto his back. From the right side of the horse let the stirrup and cinch down, making sure that the

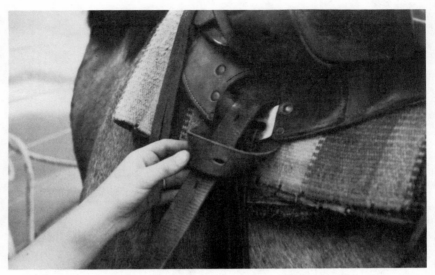

If your cinch does not have a buckle, secure the latigo in this manner.

latigo straps are not twisted and that nothing is caught under the saddle. Adjust blanket and pad so that they protrude at least one inch from under the front and back of the saddle and are hanging the same length on both sides. Slip your hand under the saddle pad at the pommel and lift up slightly. This is done so that when the saddle is tightened the pad won't apply pressure across the withers.

From the left side pull the latigo strap through the ring on the cinch. Tighten the cinch and secure the latigo, making sure that the straps in no way interfere with the animal's leg action.

The cinch should not be jerked up so tight that it could cut off the horse's air supply. A strong man could do this.

If the saddle has a back cinch, fasten it last. When removing the saddle, *always* unfasten the back cinch first. This second cinch should not be tight like the first one. Adjust it until it just touches the horse's belly.

After pulling the cinch tight, if you notice that the cinch ring on one side is higher than the other, make necessary adjustments on the right side.

A large number of horses know a way to trick their riders. They take a breath (bloat) as the handler tightens the cinch. If the rider mounts right away, he may soon discover a three-inch gap between the cinch and the horse. To alleviate this problem, walk your horse around after

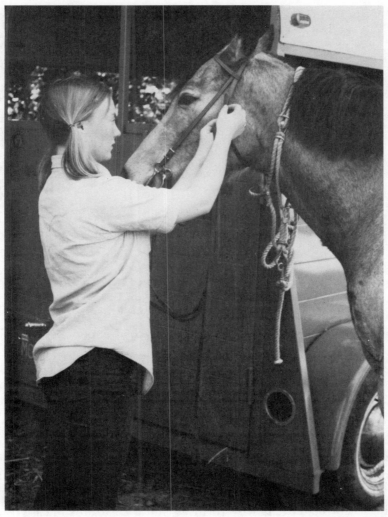

The horse at no time needs to be "untied" during bridling. Melanie is correct in holding the reins off the ground.

tightening the cinch. Then before mounting check to see if it needs to be readjusted.

With the lead rope still tied, remove the halter from the horse's face and hook it around his neck temporarily. Hold the reins so that he cannot step on them and bridle your horse. Be firm but gentle as you bridle him. Roughness here can cause many problems later. You've seen horses that wince and throw their heads every time a hand is extended

77

Whenever possible, use the shoulder and not the street.

to them. Many times this is brought on by bad experiences at bridling time.

Remove the halter and untie the lead rope. It is always a good idea to take the halter along no matter how long you plan to be out. Things can occur that make it necessary to leave your horse. It is much safer for him if he is secured, during that time, with a strong halter to a sturdy object.

Lead the horse away from fences, overhangs, eaves, low branches, or any other obstacle that could hamper the mounting process. The horse may decide to dance around a little, although this is a bad habit that should be corrected it is wise to offer him a clear area in case he does. Always mount from the horse's left side. The stirrups should be adjusted so that your knees are bent slightly when you are seated. When standing in the stirrups there should barely be room for a fist to fit between your seat and the saddle's.

Once mounted, always start your ride, whether it be in the arena or on the trail, at a walk. Just as you would find it difficult to wake up in the morning and begin vigorous exercise, your horse will need time to limber up before you can expect much from him. Athletes use limbering-up exercises before the more strenuous feats. No one can deny that a horse is an athletic creature. Always try to remember that the horse is not a machine, he is a living thing. By using the same common sense for him that you apply to yourself, you can't go too wrong.

Start out right. The reins should be held in the left hand if you are riding Western style. Try putting ten to twenty percent of your weight in the stirrups while moving at a walk. This will give you better balance and will distribute your weight at the best advantage for the horse.

Many novice riders spend most of their riding time at a run. Some of them have gotten the idea that a horse has the stamina to run for as long as the rider wants him to. Television Westerns have a lot to do with this idea. It seems that the horses used by the sheriff's posse, as well as the ones ridden by the outlaws, are galloping at full speed for days and days at a time. The impressions we get are wrong, however. The horses they use for these movies are protected by the National Humane Society. Horses are not allowed to work even as hard or for as long as their fellow human actors. The horse is allowed just so many hours on a set and then he is finished for the day. That rule holds true whether the animal was used to chase a runaway stage or to stand outside the old saloon at the hitching rail.

A good gallop can be invigorating to a horse as well as to his rider, but this should be done with caution, and not for long periods of time.

Don't run up or down hills. Be most careful about choosing a field to run in. Gopher and squirrel holes are often hidden from view by tufts of grass and weeds. When unsure of the terrain, proceed at a walk.

Traffic laws should be considered when riding in town.

Avoid soggy, muddy areas altogether. Horses have been lost in deep mud.

Don't run near busy roads, or where there is something that could possibly spook a horse.

A flat area of soft dirt in which there are no obstacles such as trees with low limbs, large rocks, etc. makes a good place for a lope or an occasional gallop. An arena is usually safe for this purpose.

Don't get into habits that will allow your horse to anticipate your moves. If you go to the same spot every day and break into a run, he might soon begin to get charged up and start prancing in excitement every time you near the place.

Likewise, don't take the same route each time you ride. Vary the ride and the gaits as much as possible. Teach the horse to do as you tell him at the time that you give the command.

Stay off of the pavement as much as possible. Not only will his hooves or shoes wear quickly, but his legs will eventually suffer from constantly being allowed to walk on pavement.

Never, never trot or run a horse on pavement of any kind.

Although most people walk their horses with the traffic, some horses behave better when facing oncoming cars. If cars tend to spook him a little as they come up behind him, he will be calmer if he can see them coming. The same holds true with bicyclists and motorcycle riders. If one is approaching you on the trail, and you feel it might startle the horse, turn him to face the two-wheeler. If the cycle rider cuts the noise on his bike, thank him. Not all of them are this courteous.

If possible, ride when traffic is lightest. If you must cross a busy street, don't take chances. Wail until it is safe. If the horse won't stand still and be patient until there is a clear spot, it may be best to dismount and lead him across the street.

Horses are not easy to see at dusk, so it is wise to stay clear of streets at this time.

Don't go into desolate areas alone. This invites problems even for the good rider. The buddy system is still best.

A foal that wants to be a tag-a-long can do so safely. Simply teach him to lead well, and he can be "ponied" along with the big guys. To do this you lead the foal as you ride the horse. Not only does this practice allow him to learn about the world around him first hand, but the exercise is very good for him. Don't plan a long trail ride for a young foal, though.

It is hard to believe that anyone would let a weanling run behind a group of riders on city streets with no means of control. But twice now I have seen this done in our town. The first time I nearly hit the little thing as he darted unexpectedly from behind the group of riders. If my car had been driven by someone who did not know to slow down and proceed with caution when horses occupy the same narrow country road, that foal would have been hit.

Don't let your horse drink from community watering troughs. Germs are transmitted in this way.

By the same token, but for slightly different reasons, don't let him graze while you are riding. It is an annoying habit to let him get into and a hard one to break. There is nothing more aggravating than to be trying to take an enjoyable ride on an ill-mannered horse who is constantly stopping to eat. As with any bad habit, prevention is the best method.

Many property owners use poisonous sprays on their unwanted weeds. Some of them are also poisonous to horses. A young friend of mine found this out the hard way. Her horse died after nibbling a neighbor's weeds.

The grass can collect in the bit and cause irritation and sores in the mouth. If you want to let your horse graze, check with the property owner. Then remove the bit, put on the halter, and let him eat. Don't let him have too much of the green stuff if he is not used to it.

When approaching an obstacle on the trail that must be jumped, some horses will balk. The rider's first thought in such cases is to lead him over the object. I do not recommend it. However, if there are no other alternatives, be very careful. Move to one side and be ready to dart out of the way of those four unsure hooves as they come flying toward you in midair.

Almost every horse owner has an occasional runaway problem. My advice here is as follows: if a group of horses escape from the pasture, catch the easiest one first. Don't hold out hoping to capture the hard-to-catch ones because you know that the others are a cinch to snag.

The best thing to do is to keep him so secure that he won't get out. The dangers to a horse in civilization are too high. So is the fee you pay animal control if they catch him before you do. So is the veterinarian's bill high if the horse should get injured while running rampant—not to mention the bill you might receive from a neighbor for the damage your horse has done to his property. Don't take chances. Be sure he is properly secured.

Any cleared, flat space can become a practice arena.

If a horse somehow breaks loose while on a trail ride, don't chase him. That will just make him run faster in most cases. Horses are herd-bound animals. That is, they do not like to be away from their horse friends. Although a horse may run merrily past you at a swift pace, head high, tail flying in obvious delight, once he rounds a corner where he can't see his buddies, his attitude changes. He will more than likely peer around the bend at the group in a very few minutes. With little encouragement his mischief will end and he will rejoin the trail ride. If, however, the horse doesn't come back, some of the riding party will have to go in search of him. Follow his trail as an Indian brave would, noting the direction of his tracks. Move in on him slowly so as not to startle him into running from you.

If you see a saddled, riderless horse heading in your direction, by all means block his path in an effort to stop him.

What if you are on the runaway? Well, first I'd advise you not to let yourself get into that position. Don't encourage an unfamiliar horse into a dead run. If he has run away with you before, or you think he has the tendency to do so, keep him checked (under control) at all times. You'll soon be able to feel him before he plans one of his runaway tricks and will be able to check him right away.

If you somehow still manage to become involved with a horse who will not stop, stay with him. Reach down and grab one rein close to the bit. Then pull him around in a small circle. Since a horse cannot physically run fast in a small circle, he'll have to slow down and eventually stop. He will probably be worked up after this display of speed, so proceed at a walk, keeping close control of the horse until he has calmed down.

We've all seen a horse balk and show signs of near hysteria over the idea of crossing a trickling creek that wouldn't come up as high as a mosquito's navel. The rider seems perfectly justified in forcing a horse to complete this request, doesn't he?

We've also seen horses refuse to pass a harmless bush on the trail only to learn later that a rattlesnake lay coiled inside it. The same horse will step right over a rattler that is stretched across the road in plain sight without a thought. The point is, contrary to some reports, a horse does not always know best. Some people have the misconceived notion that if the horse will eventually do what he is asked to do, it is of no danger to him. This is not true. We have to decide for him what is wise and what isn't. This statement is proved by the horse who tried to walk across a cattle guard in Nevada at her rider's request. The poor mare did as her rider asked and ended up in a most embarrassing and painful predicament. Three hours later, under a sedative, she was freed from the grasp of the metal slats.

A red ribbon tied to the tail has become the sign of a horse that is known to kick.

While riding in a group it is best to stay together, but not too close. A horse that is known to kick other horses should be marked with a red ribbon tied to the tail. This will remind other riders to be extra cautious where this horse is concerned.

If someone stops to tighten his cinch, open and close a gate, or clean out a hoof, the others should also stop. Wait until everyone is mounted before riding off.

Try to refrain from using universal clucking noises and other phrases to urge your horse on. Other horses might respond to your commands, knocking their riders off balance.

Point out rocks, low branches, and other trail hazards to the rider behind you.

Never lope on the trail without prior warning and a nod of approval from everyone else. One running horse can stampede the whole group of horses.

Close all gates found closed and leave open all gates found that way. There was a recent case of four horses who died when the gate to their water supply was closed. The trail rider thought they were doing a good deed by closing the gate they found open.

Don't ride across land that is under cultivation.

While visiting, tie your horse where he can't eat or trample the landscape. If he leaves a pile in the yard, borrow a shovel and clean it for the homeowner.

Respect other people's rights and property. Not everyone likes horses. Those who don't can make a neighborhood pretty miserable for those who do. You will be doing everyone who has horses a big favor if you will observe these rules while riding. Do not ride through your neighbor's yard unless you have specific permission. This does not mean that you can do it because your friends can do it. You must have permission of your own. Be courteous when someone asks you to remove a pile of manure that your horse dropped. This will happen. In fact in some cities, you can get a ticket for littering if your horse does "his thing" on the streets. If you let your dog tag along with you, keep him out of the neighbor's yard, too. Dust upsets some people. If there is laundry drying on the line, don't run past and cause dust to fly all over the clean wash.

Don't run cattle or horses in a pasture.

Don't feed or water someone else's horse. The horse could be on medication that requires the omission of water for several hours. If in doubt, however, ask. A pony near us died when a misunderstanding

Dona is lungeing her horse.

between the two owners took place. A passing rider, hiker, or biker, inquiring as to the pony's lack of water and food might have saved him from his fate of starvation.

Here is a list of "cute" things that horses do, that can turn into dangerous things.

1. Nibbling.
2. Dancing around while you mount.
3. Putting ears back and squealing at other horses.
4. Pawing the ground.
5. Wanting to run back to the barn.
6. Chewing on the toe of the rider's boot.
7. Chewing on equipment or corral fences.
8. Trotting when you prefer to walk.

Be consistent in your demands. Cue him the same every time. A horse is basically willing. He will try to oblige if he understands what you want of him. Communication is a very large problem in the United States. People who speak the same language sometimes have trouble communicating effectively. You can readily see how a problem in understanding one another can occur between horse and human.

Don't demand too much at one time when a horse is in a learning session. Two or three ten-minute sessions in one day will offer much better results than will daily sessions of forty-five minutes on the same topic.

Practice makes perfect, but give him a break. Vary his activities.

Teach the animal to work on a longe line for those days when you can't ride. This method is also used for exercising young horses and for readying a more spirited horse for riding. To longe a horse you will need a halter, 30' rope, and a long, buggy-type whip. The object is to get the horse to walk, jog, and lope in a circle around you.

To longe a horse to the left, hold the longe line in the left hand and the buggy whip in the right. Touch him on the hind legs with the whip as you urge him forward and in a circle around you.

Gradually feed out the rope as his circle becomes bigger.

Do not hit the horse with the whip. Do not wave it around at him. Hold it at waist height. Snap it sharply on the ground when he fails to respond to a command.

To give him the idea to stop when you say "whoa", hold the whip in front of his chest.

Have him change direction from time to time so that he won't become too bored.

A horse that is getting a rest from his daily riding should be longed for thirty minutes. When the horse is learning what longing is all about, work him for ten to fifteen minutes at a time.

A horse is in poor condition if he is too fat, too skinny, or if he tires easily. To ease such an animal into a good work program, ride him at a walk forty-five minutes a day for a week. Then walk him forty-five minutes and jog fifteen minutes each day for six weeks. A conditioned horse should work from one-and-a-half to two hours each day at a walk, jog, and lope to keep him that way.

Don't punish a horse for his natural behavior such as spooking. Be calm and speak to him in reassuring tones. An excited horse will only become more so if his handler also loses his cool.

Always walk the horse the last fifteen minutes of his working sessions to start the cooling out process. Cool the horse out thoroughly before putting him away.

If he is very sweaty, remove the excess moisture with a sweat scraper. Rub him down with a damp cloth to remove the sweat from back, legs, chest, and head. A day sheet might be used to keep the cool air off of his damp body. Walk him until he is dry and cool. The chest will be the last place to cool down. You can figure that if his chest is dry and cool, so is he.

It is best not to feed him for thirty minutes after he has been put away, but he can have water at this point.

Most horse-oriented accidents are the handler's fault. Think about it. Consider all of the accidents you know about that involved a horse and decide how many of them were really his fault.

Some people mistakes that I've seen that have caused injury or death to either horse or handler or both are:

1. Riding bareback.
2. Riding with or using faulty equipment.
3. Walking up behind a horse.
4. Getting into a pen with a mare and her new foal.
5. Taking an inexperienced horse or one that is out of shape on a strenuous ride.
6. Allowing a horse to nibble clothing.
7. Swatting an unaware horse on the rump.
8. Tying a horse to an object that is not sturdy.
9. Not keeping extra feed out of reach of gluttonous horses.
10. Not fastening the gate on the pasture or corral.
11. Leaving harmful objects in animal's corrals.
12. Pushing a fatigued horse to keep going.
13. Not keeping electrical cords out of reach of nosey horses.
14. Putting horses that aren't familiar with one another, together.
15. Forcing a horse to perform a task that is impossible or dangerous.
16. A novice riding too spirited a horse.
17. Poor horse management in general.
18. Poor feed program.
19. Trying to doctor a seriously ill or injured horse yourself instead of calling the veterinarian.

One horse is enough responsibility for a beginner. I do not recommend that a novice go into any sort of a breeding program.

The idea of having a foal in the backyard is beautiful, but the reality of it isn't always so nice.

The facilities must be altered to accommodate a youngster. The cost of feed will increase as a more structured and detailed diet will be necessary for the mare in foal, for the nursing mare, and for the foal as he grows.

Veterinarian's bills will probably double. It is only logical because, instead of one, there will be two horses. There is the mare care prior to her foaling and after, there is the care of the foal when he is born and as

The prospect of a "backyard" foal may be irresistable, but often requires more effort than is realized.

he grows. If he is a colt, there is the problem of deciding whether or not to have him gelded. If you don't, a separate and very sturdy pen will be required to contain your stallion. If you do, there is an added expense of the operation and the care afterwards.

There is the little fellow's training to consider, extra equipment in his size, which must be replaced as he grows.

There is also added responsibility. Foals are cute. They look harmless and innocent. But their nature, as with any young thing, is playful, unpredictable, and sometimes downright ornery. They can cause serious injury with a whimsical display of affection.

Young horses are even more accident prone than grown horses. It takes a near perfect facility to keep a colt or filly from harming itself.

For those of you who are still determined to raise a backyard foal, here are some tips that could help.

A normal mare can have her first foal by age four and can be bred every year until age nineteen or so. A mare that has been barren (not had a foal) for a couple of years is much harder to settle (become pregnant) than one which has foaled every year.

Mares come in heat every twenty-one days. An average heat lasts anywhere from four to eight days.

If your mare is in 'heat' she will urinate frequently. She will raise her tail and flex the vulva. And she'll have a noticeable discharge from the vagina. Some mares are much more obvious when in heat than others. You may have to take a quiet mare to a stallion to get a noticeable reaction from her.

Make sure your mare is in good condition before subjecting her to being bred. She should not be overweight or undernourished. It is best to have a veterinarian check her general health prior to breeding her.

Choose a stallion with care. His conformation, disposition, general health and resistancy to disease should be taken into consideration. If you must breed, at least do it intelligently.

It is against the law in many places to breed horses in public. That also means that you can be fined for leaving a mare and a stallion together in a pen where passersby can observe them.

It's best to aid the two horses in their relationship. They could hurt one another if left alone. There should be three people present: someone to hold the mare, one to hold the stallion, and one to make sure that the job is getting done properly. Yes, in some cases the stallion will need help in entering the mare.

When the breeding is over, walk the mare so she does not have a chance to urinate. It sometimes helps to spray cool water on the vulva to encourage her to tighten up.

The gestation period is eleven months, or 340 days from conception to birth.

Watch for a heat period in twenty-one days after breeding. If she doesn't have one, chances are she "took."

In fifty days from the mating, a veterinarian's check can be performed. Ask at that time about your mare's prenatal care.

Another veterinarian's check may be necessary when the mare is five or six months along. A mare can abort without you knowing it, because she can absorb the fetus within her.

Every authority on the subject of horses has a different list of symptoms one should watch for that will indicate the exact day a mare will foal. Some of them say that when the udder is full and distended the mare is just two to six weeks from her foaling date. Seven to ten days prior to foaling, the muscles around the tail begin to be noticeably relaxed and give the appearance of being concave. The stomach will drop. Four to six days before the birth the teats fill out and milk might begin to drip from them in large quantity. Some mares "wax up." This means that a waxy substance appears on the ends of the teats. These little plugs are supposed to show up two to four days ahead.

Restlessness, frequent urination, and sweating are all signs that should be present in your mare just hours before the foal is to make an appearance. These and all other symptoms mentioned are general. Some mares show all of these before foaling and others may have none of them.

The point is, the foal will be born when it is ready whether the moon is full, it is the first of the month, or its mother's teats wax up or not.

Once the wobbly legged creature is living and breathing on his own, it is wise to have a veterinarian check him over and administer a tetanus shot.

The mare will also need a checkup. It must be determined if the afterbirth was completely expelled by the mare. If a piece of it is left inside she could become seriously ill in less than twelve hours.

From his first day until he is around six months old, the foal will rely on his mother for the majority of his nourishment and protection. Your responsibility during this time includes supplementing the mare's milk as your vet suggests, keeping him safe and secure inside his corral, having him wormed every eight weeks, having his hooves cared for as your farrier suggests, and not teaching him any bad habits that will be hard to break as he grows bigger and stronger.

As they mature, colts or fillies can become hard to handle. You will be happier with a horse you can use than with one that is so spoiled that the family is afraid to take him from the corral. Anywhere from three to six months with a trainer should make your three-year-old a well-mannered horse that the whole family can ride and enjoy.

Ride your horse defensively. It is recommended that you drive your car defensively, and watch out for the other guy, and it is also smart to ride your horse with the same attitude. Youngsters may ride bikes lickity split past you or fly kites without regard for your horse's fears. People in cars sometimes honk their horns or yell as they drive past you, just for the kick of watching the horse's reaction.

Remember that not everyone knows the horse species as you do. Small children and sometimes their parents need to be reminded (or told) that certain things are just not done around a horse. This is part of your responsibility. Keep your horse and the people he comes in contact with safe.

When you buy a horse, you are not just an individual with a horse. You are a representative of all horseback riders. You owe it to the horse community to be a responsible horse person. All horse owners and riders are being judged by your actions. A few inconsiderate riders can ruin the reputation of all of them.

7 WHEN THE SHOW BUG BITES

It is not unusual for the beginner rider to become interested in the local horse shows. And why not? There are many opportunities open in the field of showing even for the novice.

Sharing is one of the wonderful things about life. People who have spent many hours fixing up beautiful old cars enjoy displaying them for show. Purebred dog and cat owners enter the show ring with their best animals. It is not so unusual for the horse owner to want to exhibit the horse of which he is so proud.

Shows are a perfect place to enjoy the company of other horse

Before entering the show, lessons are a good idea.

Riding apparel for show is designed to give a neat, uncluttered appearance.

lovers. The localized play days offer competitive events for people of all ages and of varying degrees of horse know-how. Horse shows are a great way for the entire family to spend time together. The main objective of the show sponsors are to promote horsemanship and to provide fun for everyone involved.

An important question asked by many prospective show people is, "Do I need a trainer?" This, of course, is up to the individual. Unless this person is unusually perceptive and observant and can pick up the correct ways of the arena by simply watching the winners, I'd suggest that he take some lessons.

The first step is to decide how extensive the training should be. Explain to the trainer your previous experience in riding and what your immediate goals are. The trainer will take it from there. He will most likely ask you to ride. He'll watch your form. He'll observe the horse's response to your cues. From this demonstration he will know more precisely what points to stress in his instruction.

In most cases there are at least three methods of lessons open to a person and his horse. There are the weekly lessons for which the student is charged by the hour. There is a plan where the horse is boarded and the rider is to come each day to take a lesson. It is most likely that the payments will be made monthly with this arrangement. The more professional show people turn their horses over to a trainer. He works the horse every single day. The trainer is usually responsible for taking the horse to the shows. He does the grooming and all of the other work involved. The owner need only climb aboard, ride out, and win the class.

Before entering a show, attend a few of them. Observe the clothing the riders wear. Watch the constant winners closely and practice the things that you notice. Take your horse to a few shows to get him used to being around other horses.

Decide which of the classes you would most like to participate in. Listed here are some of the more familiar events offered at Western shows and play days. By the way, *play day* is usually the term given a small show that is mostly for the local people. Training gear is usually permitted. These are less professional shows for a wider range of riders.

Showmanship is a class that gives the handler the opportunity to show a well-behaved horse that perhaps lacks conformation. The handlers present the animals at hand. That is, they lead the horses into the arena instead of ride them. The handler is being judged as to how well he (or she) can show the horse. The judge will check closely for any flaws in grooming. Bot eggs, dust flying when patted, an unattended wound, tangled mane, grown-out bridle path, and ragged, uncared for hooves will all go against the handler in the showmanship class.

A proper halter is a must. The lead is held in the right hand with the extra coils held flat in the left. The handler always belongs on the left side of the horse, except when the judge is on that side. The handler never stands between the judge and the horse. The handler never turns his back on the judge, unless specifically asked to do so. The horse and the handler should retain an aura of alertness at all times. The judge will want to see the way the horse moves at a jog. It takes practice to get the horse to jog next to you on a lead. Another thing that takes constant, repetitive practice is teaching the horse to square up, or to stand squarely with his weight distributed evenly on all four feet.

Teaching the horse to "square up" for halter and showmanship classes requires patience.

Two competitors in a Western equitation class.

A horse in the left lead.

A horse in the right lead.

95

This horse is cautious as he approaches an obstacle in the Western trail course.

The halter class, although presented just as the showmanship class, is judged more on the conformation of the horse than on anything else. Now most people think that their horse is flawlessly beautiful. Maybe he is to you, but there are certain standards that denote perfect conformation in a horse. The judge knows what these standards are and it is his job to choose the horse that comes the closest.

Cleanliness and condition are also important in a halter class. As with any other form of showing, it is important for the handler/rider to be clean and neat too.

The Western pleasure and equitation classes are riding classes. The rider must ask his horse to walk, jog, and lope in both directions of the arena at the announcer's request. A smooth-moving, well-behaved horse will be what this judge is looking for. Leads are extremely important here. As you will note in the diagram, a horse in a lope can lead with either front leg. When his left side is to the inside of the arena (away from the fence) he should be reaching out farther with the left leg. In other words, he should always lead with the inside leg. It may take some practice to get a green horse, or one that has been allowed to take the lead he wants, to learn to take the correct lead on command. A trainer can be most helpful here.

The rider who sits tall, looks relaxed, and does very little moving in the saddle gives a good overall appearance to a pleasure horse. Even the smoothest horse can look rough if the rider pumps, jerks, and slumps in the saddle.

The basic difference between the pleasure and equitation class is that the horse is more important in the pleasure class, and in equitation it is the rider.

The rider is often asked to dismount and to mount again in the equitation class, and most likely he will also be asked to back his horse in either pleasure or equitation.

The trail class provides fun and variety for a rider and a horse. The rider is required to follow a certain course as he takes his horse through a series of obstacles. The course may include a bridge, gate, logs to walk over without touching, a tire to pivot around, a sack of noisy cans, a jump, barrels to back around, and a mailbox to side-pass up to. As a rule each horse/rider team is given ten points per obstacle at the start of this event. Points are then taken off for each balk, mistake, or for not following the rules explicitly.

Western Riding classes are fun to watch and rather complicated for the beginner to participate in. This class includes a series of lead changes and figure eights.

Stock Seat is similar to Western Pleasure and Western Equitation classes, but the judge will usually request individual work.

Gymkhana events are exciting for the spectators as well as for the riders.

97

Stock Horse classes are popular with the cowboys. The quick spins and sliding stops require many hours of practice and in most cases a horse of special ability.

Gymkhana events are usually the most popular for the beginner or for the person who has a limited amount of money to spend for riding attire and flashy equipment. These speed events draw people who don't even know the back of the horse from the front as well as very accomplished riders. Parents of children who run barrels chew their fingernails as their child flies from one end of the arena to the other, closely hugging the obstacles without tipping them over. People who prefer pleasure riding consider gymkhana riders either extremely brave or slightly crazy. Once a child or an adult breaks into these speed events, however, he is hooked. In their estimation there is nothing to compare with the feeling they get from this exciting sport.

Some people ride pleasure classes and gymkhana with the same horse. Not all horses have the temperament to handle these two extremes, however.

Experts tell me that a horse does not have to possess terrific speed to become a good gymkhana horse. All that is really required in a horse is consistency and the ability to respond quickly to the cues of the rider.

If this fast, dirt-flying sport is one you'd like to try, start out slowly. You'll need a place where you can practice. Set up barrels (or poles) and walk your horse through the course to give him the idea of what you want him to do. Do this once or twice every day for several days. Next jog him through the course, making sure to stay close to the obstacles as you turn each one. It won't take him long to get the idea.

Practice will be necessary, but most trainers agree that it is not a good idea to do this practicing at a run more than a few times a day. The horse does not need to learn speed, it is coordination, consistency, and the desire and ability to respond that you are after.

To keep the shows from becoming strictly competitive, sometimes a fun event is held.

The Egg and Spoon Ride is one such fun event. Each rider is given a regular kitchen spoon and a raw egg. The participants are then asked to walk, jog, and lope as usual around the arena with the spoon and egg in one hand the last person to drop his egg is the winner.

The Boot Race is also fun. Everyone is asked to remove his boots. The boots are then placed at the far end of the arena. On the "go" sign, all participants ride to the pile of boots, dismount and begin the search for their own. The rider who makes it to the finish line with both of his boots on his feet is declared the winner.

To be a properly outfitted gymkhana rider, you will need a comfortable, lightweight saddle, Western boots, long-sleeved shirt, slacks, belt, tie, and in some cases a helmet. The bit should not be a severe one. Some people who ride both pleasure and gymkhana have two bits. Bosels or hackamore bits are popular with gymkhana riders. Some people swear by the snaffle bit for the speed events.

For the pleasure classes, plan to have slacks, long-sleeved Western shirt, Western saddle, bridle, and showy saddle blanket. Chaps are optional in play days. However, if most of the people in your area wear them, it would be wise to invest in a pair.

A riata (or reata) is also a requirement to complete the Western outfit. This is a small coil of rawhide that ties to the saddle. Hobbles are required when the reins are the closed type.

For larger shows the competition is greater in all areas, including riding, equipment, and attire. The equitation suit or Western suit with a jacket are the popular clothing for women in more professional shows. Chaps are required for the big shows. Chaps have a way of lasting forever. Many times people tire of their old ones or outgrow them. Very often they will advertise them for sale at a reasonable price. Watch horse-club newsletters, bulletin boards, and the newspaper for a good pair of used chaps in your size. If they fit, but the color is wrong, you can dye them at home. Instructions are in chapter 10. Another way of getting a good pair of chaps for relatively little cost is to make them. Instructions are in chapter 10. So is a pattern for the popular equitation suit.

Be practical in choosing show-riding attire. The chaps should be of a fairly neutral shade that complements the color of the horse. The more neutral the color, the more choices available in the equitation suit fabric. The suit can be loud or soft shades—that is up to the individual. Some people believe that a bright color will more readily catch the judge's eye. Here again the color of the horse should be considered.

The boots, hat, belt, tie, and chaps should be the same color. It is not necessary, but this is my suggestion to those who are in the market for a complete outfit.

A straw hat is fine for play days, but you'll notice that few are present in the arena at the larger shows. For these shows felt hats or the new crushable straw hats are the most popular.

I've seen some striking combinations of riding attire and horse colors recently. I loved the black horse with the deep lavender saddle blanket. His rider wore an equitation suit to match the blanket and accented the outfit with dark purple chaps and hat. The little gal who wears a light pink suit, dark pink chaps and hat really knows how to complement the color of her light sorrel Appy. A change in these outfits would most likely mean the expense of new chaps, so the following examples are probably more practical. My daughter liked her yellow gingham suit and chocolate chaps with her Appy. The navy chaps and baby blue suit are striking on a gray or white horse.

If your future plans include the big show circuit, start accumulating silver now. You'll need silver for your horn, a silver back plate, silver screws to hold your stirrups, silver corner plates both for front and back, a silver bit, silver pieces on the headstall and reins, and of course a few pieces on the chaps and perhaps the hat. Without purchasing a new saddle, this will amount to approximately $400 to $500. It is nice to know that the equipment won't depreciate much. So you can consider this an investment.

There is one more sad fact, however. You won't be able to use old Molly, your faithful first horse who has been teaching you to ride for these past few years. A new, sharp-looking, intelligent, most probably very expensive horse will have to take Molly's place. If the horse is well trained, he will cost considerably more. If not, you'll put the money into him anyway to get him well trained.

Big-time showing is highly competitive and very expensive. The

This participant has a chance to win. Her attire is suitable, her hair is neatly groomed, and her entry number will not blow and flap around.

young girl who came in third last year in the Pacific Coast circuit confesses that it cost her family around $20,000 for the year. That is just entry fees, trainer, and traveling expenses.

Now that you are thoroughly convinced that the big shows are not for you, at least right now, let's go back to the play day, or smaller show.

As I said before, watch some shows before entering one. Ask for a copy of the rules that particular organization follows. Request to be put on the mailing list so that you will know when and where each show will be and the classes that are offered. A notice with this information should arrive a week prior to the show. Entry fees for play days are usually anywhere from $2 to $4 for the entire day, or $.50 to $1 per class. The larger shows usually charge from $2.50 per class clear up to $20 or more. Decide which classes you are interested in and practice those every day.

On the day before the show, after your practice session, start readying your mount for his big day.

Make sure his bridle path is trimmed and neat looking. Trim the hair around the hooves and fetlocks. Remove all bot eggs (the yellow dots that stick to his chest and legs). We use a razor blade to scrape these stubborn eggs loose. Trim all of the long hairs (whiskers) from the muzzle and chin either with clippers or scissors. Likewise trim away the

This is a handy way to carry grooming aids to the horse show.

long hairs inside the ear. Don't get carried away here. Simply fold the ear in half lengthwise holding the outside of the ear. Trim away those inside hairs that are sticking out.

The next step is a complete bath. After drying him thoroughly, apply a day sheet (unless he is used to a night blanket) and put him away.

Your next chore will be to clean the saddle and bridle. Use silver polish to make your belt buckle and other silver pieces sparkle.

If the saddle pad is really filthy you'd better wash it, otherwise, just brush it vigorously until all loose particles are removed. Wash the saddle blanket if necessary.

Wipe or brush the dust from your hat and check over your riding outfit for any missing buttons, rips, etc. Don't forget to polish your boots.

On the day of the show, get up extra early and toss the horse his ration of feed.

After a good breakfast for yourself, start getting dressed. I find that it is wise to cover a clean equitation suit with an old pair of overalls while working with my horse.

For a woman, the hair should be pulled back neatly into a tight braid or bun. The hair should not be left to flop and fly around.

Load the equipment into the car. Make sure you haven't forgotten anything. You'll need a saddle, saddle pads and blanket, bucket for water and to carry grooming equipment in, brushes, hoof pick, damp sponge, grooming cloth, fly repellent, mane and tail comb, scissors, and bridle. Put the chaps and hat into a covered box or plastic bag.

When your horse has finished eating, bring him to the grooming place. Remove the blanket and check him over for dirt he might have acquired overnight. His lower legs may need to be washed again, especially if he has white stockings. Wipe his face with the damp sponge. Clean off his hooves. Some people like to give their animal a real finished look by applying black shoe polish to his hooves. To do this, stand him on pavement. Apply a liquid polish and make him stand until the hooves are dry.

Some horses have rather unruly mane and tails. If yours does, try wrapping the tail with an Ace bandage until show time. Likewise, a towel can be pinned around the horse's neck to hold the dampened mane hairs smooth.

Once on the show grounds, hot-foot it to the entry booth to enter the classes you desire. Ask how long you have before your first class is to begin and gauge your time by that.

Brush any newly accumulated dust off of the horse's body and face. Comb the mane and tail and double-check for dirt, bots, etc.

Saddle him up and get on him to limber him up for the show. Most arenas have a warm-up area. Use it. Walk, jog, and lope, keeping calm and quiet, and this will encourage the horse to do the same.

If possible find someone who will help hold your horse while you put on your chaps. This person will also be needed to pull down the legs of your chaps after you are on the horse and to wipe the dust off of your boots.

Now you are ready to go into the ring. It is best to move the horse around prior to entering the arena. When your class is approaching, start walking him so that he will be well limbered and alert each time he performs.

This is important whether you are a pleasure, trail, gymkhana, or English rider.

Other things to remember if you are interested in showing are:

1. Be prompt for your class.
2. While in the ring, don't crowd or cut off another rider.
3. Stay next to the rail as much as possible.
4. Stay in the open as much as possible so the judge might see you.
5. To get away from a crowded situation, circle toward the center of the ring, at the proper gait, and ease into an open area. Do not interfere with another rider.
6. Keep your horse under control at all times.
7. Don't run your horse in the congested warm-up arena. People and horses have been known to get hurt this way.
8. Don't take your horse near the bleachers, where the spectators are or near the food booth. Small children usually attend horse shows and many of them have not learned how to behave around horses.
9. Be courteous and a good sport. Be happy when you win and vow to work harder when you don't.
10. Remember you are simply asking for the opinion of the judge, by riding under him. Even though you may not agree, accept his decision with a smile.
11. Sometimes there is the opportunity between classes to ask the judge where you fell down in the class. This information can be invaluable.

Judging.

A contestant happily accepting an award.

To help you place you should learn to tell what lead your horse is in without having to ask someone or to peek over his shoulder to see for yourself. This takes practice, but it makes a lot of difference in a class. Which contestant would you be more apt to place? Susie, who leans across her horse's neck to see which leg is in the lead? Or Margaret, who sits tall as she cues her horse into the correct lead?

While riding a class, if your horse does pick up the wrong lead, by all means correct it right away. The judge will be much more impressed by a person who recognizes the mistake and corrects it than one who rides an entire class in the wrong lead.

I mentioned before the importance of a smooth, well-groomed appearance without flying pony tails (other than the horse's), cute dangling hair ribbons, or blousy, floppy clothes. The entry number, too, should be made to conform. Cut it down until just the number is on the cardboard. Then pin it at both the top and the bottom, whether it is to be pinned on you or the saddle pad.

Don't chew gum. Kids, especially, will enter the arena with a huge wad of bubble gum. They plan to keep it hidden as they ride. It isn't long until their concentration becomes so intense that they forget their promise to themselves, and to Mom, and the jaws start unconciously working that gum like crazy.

Everyone loves a good sport. Of course you have worked hard to prepare for this show, and for what purpose? To bring home every prize? Is that what is important to you, the ribbons and cheap little trophies? Or are you in this for the fun of it? Keep the correct perspective here. Do your absolute best and get out of it what you are in it for: the enjoyment of the companionship of your beloved horse and of those, who like you, love horses.

This is a good idea for any rider or spectator to remember. Never make derogatory remarks about a horse or rider. You never know who may be sitting next to you.

8 TAKE HIM THERE SAFELY

How do you plan to get to the show? If it is close enough, by all means ride. But if you are stuck many miles away from the arena, and you want to show regularly, you'd better consider buying a trailer.

Most people get plenty of use from their horse trailers. Some even use a trailer to haul their horse along on summer vacations. When you finally have access to a trailer you'll soon find yourself accepting all sorts of invitations for you and your horse.

There are many types, models, and prices available in the horse

Always inspect a trailer before buying it.

trailer market. I'm not going to pretend to be a salesperson, but there are a few points that I think are important to the prospective buyer.

First of all, even if you have only one horse, I would definitely urge you to buy a two-horse trailer. Even though you may doubt it now, things do happen to necessitate two spaces in a trailer.

Consider a used trailer first. Check it out just as you would a used car. How are the tires? Is it badly in need of a paint job? Are there any rusty spots? Does the trailer have a step up or a ramp for the horse to enter and exit from? Check the loading gate situation. Is it easy to open and close? It certainly should be if a woman or youngster is to be handling it. What about the butt chains (or bars)? A trailer must have these to prevent a horse from crashing out on top of you as you open the doors and lower the ramp for him to exit. These butt bars also prevent him from rubbing his tail raw on the metal or wooden doors.

Preferably a manger should be available. And wire mesh dividers are necessary to keep the horses' heads on their respective sides. There need to be strong tie hooks in the front on both sides. Is the trailer floor sturdy? Don't forget that it must be strong enough to stand up under 2,500 pounds or so. Sometimes the urine can cause floorboards to rot.

The floor should be covered with a nonskid mat of some sort.

The inside of the trailer must be free of sharp edges, splintered wood, and other hazards. A center divider is optional. Some horsepeople

When you have a horse trailer there is no limit to the places you can ride.

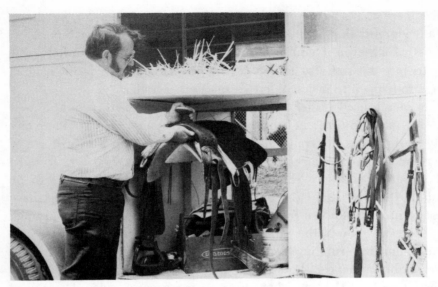

This is an ideal setup for transporting tack.

won't trailer without one, and others prefer to remove the divider. Be leery of a divider that is solid to the floor. A large horse will find it difficult to get the leg room he needs and will have trouble standing in this trailer. Removal of the lower half of the divider usually alleviates this problem.

Some trailers do not have brakes. This too, is a matter of preference. For in-town driving on flat roads, brakes may not be needed. For long trips and mountain travel, however, brakes are a must.

If you plan to do much traveling in the back country, check the way the trailer sits. How high off the ground is it? You'll have trouble maneuvering one that is only six inches off the ground, over rut-riddled country roads.

A trailer with springs under each wheel is preferred. Tandem wheels are best for the most equal distribution of weight. These are the most important things for consideration when seeking the right trailer for you and your equine friend.

Here are some extras that you may or may not want. Most trailers will feature padding around the manger, but some will even include padded side walls. A saddle rack in the storage compartment is a nice convenience. Inside lights are available in some trailers. Lights do come in handy if you must load a horse in the dark. A horse hates to go into a trailer when he can't see where he is going and what he will encounter

With proper training, a horse can learn to go willingly into the trailer.

once there. Car lights or a flashlight shining from behind the horse sometimes helps in this type of situation.

The larger rigs sometimes include a dressing room and even a place to sleep. These trailers are very handy to use for out-of-town shows, or for following the rodeo circuit, but they are usually just too fancy for the backyard rider.

A strong hitch on a car or pickup of suitable horse power is very important. Beware of the hitch setup that is designed to pull a small utility trailer. If you are having the hitch put on, stress to the mechanics the weight of the load you'll be pulling. A safety chain should also be part of the hitch.

Then there are large stock trucks that can carry anywhere from four to six horses. Hunters and horsepackers like this mode of transporting horses. Many stock trucks can be easily converted into flat beds for hauling hay on.

Pickup owners sometimes find a stock rack for their trucks very convenient. If the truck is too light, however, the weight of the horses will affect the way it handles.

If your horse has never been inside a trailer, you may have some fun to look forward to. Be quiet and gentle but firm. Lead him to the open trailer and let him get used to its appearance. He'll no doubt sniff and snort around as he examines it. When he seems to be comfortable with

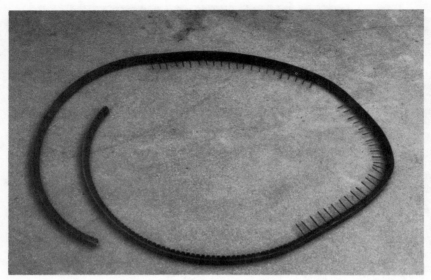

This tack collar can be used as a last resort in loading a stubborn horse.

the presence of the trailer, lead him to the ramp (or step up). It is not wise to enter a trailer with a horse, but it may be necessary at times. Do not enter the stall that you are putting him into unless there is an escape door for you to exit from. If no escape hatch is available, step into the trailer on the opposite side of the divider, and from there lead your horse in.

Once he's in fasten the butt bar. Next tie the halter rope short and secure, and then close the door. The small doors on the front are designed for you to reach the horse to tie him. Don't try to do this from inside the trailer. In fact, ideally, you should never have to step even one foot inside that trailer as you load a horse. It may be necessary at first, but do it with extreme caution.

If you didn't find this loading task as easy as I made it sound, here are some suggestions.

If there are two horses, load the veteran traveler first. The novice horse may just follow his lead.

Have some hay in the manger to help entice him.

You might try coaxing a stubborn horse in with this method. Station one person at each end of a twelve-foot rope. Line the horse up to the trailer opening. As someone leads the horse toward the ramp the two people with the rope, who are on opposite sides of the horse, should bring the rope up until it touches the horse's rear end. Keeping the rope against the horse's rear, walk with him and ease him into the trailer.

I've been told that another foolproof method of getting a horse into a trailer is to use a horse blanket in much the same way as the rope. Fold the blanket on the bias. Without spooking the horse with it, bring it up behind him and use it to force him in as with the rope.

Another method you might try is to loop a rope around the chest (behind the front legs). Draw the end of the rope through a slipknot at the chest and up through the halter. When pressure is applied to this lead rope, it should cause him to move forward and into the trailer.

The method used by many old-timers is the tack collar. This collar consists of an eight-foot strip of tire rubber into which many little nails have been driven. The very points of the nails are then snipped off leaving only stubby ends. This device is held by two people behind the horse. The collar should be brought toward to horse's rump. Gently apply the pressure of the blunt nails against the rump. The horse should move anywhere but backwards. This method can work well and humanely. Do not abuse it, or use this as a means of punishment.

Another workable solution to get him into the trailer is to flick him on the lower legs with the end of a buggy-type whip. No violence please, simply touch the legs. This will cause him to step forward and into the trailer.

Many people like to get a solid grip on the lead rope so that they can hold that horse in case he pulls back. I've never seen a man yet who could hold a horse who is bent on pulling back. Use common sense. You've got to convince that horse that he should go into that trailer. No amount of people can bodily force a full-grown obstinate horse into the trailer.

May I suggest that, although these are tried and true methods, they should not all be used in one day. If you must go through every one of these ideas, your horse will be so upset and cranky by the end of the day that you may never get him in. I would like to see you try one of the methods that you prefer and perhaps one other if it fails. But it is best to rest the horse and try again another day, or perhaps later the same day if he becomes too nervous and upset.

If time is unimportant, there is yet another way to solve this trailer-loading problem. Park the trailer inside the horse's pen and feed him from it. He'll soon become used to the sound of his hooves echoing on the hollow trailer floor. He'll think nothing of being closed in by three walls and a low roof. His memories of the trailer will become pleasant ones.

By displaying confidence yourself it may rub off on your horse. As you lead him up to the trailer ramp, do it with assurance.

When you finally get him to load on command, you may want to take the horse on a short ride. Do this a few times before attempting a trip of great distance.

When trailering a mare and foal, tie the mare in and let the little fellow move around on his own. He may need to be lifted into the trailer. If his mother goes first, he will most likely follow, however.

It is not a particularly good idea to trailer a horse with his saddle on. If he isn't used to having this bulky chunk of leather on him while in the trailer, he could get spooked when the saddle rubs the sides of the trailer as he rides.

The other problem is that the saddle can get terribly nicked and scratched from scraping against the trailer walls.

If you must put your horse in under his saddle, tie up the stirrups so that they won't be flopping around.

Don't load him with the bridle on. It is very easy to catch a strap or buckle on the divider, the manger, etc.

Drive with caution when you are hauling a horse behind you. Turn corners slowly and smoothly. Avoid bumps in the road. Brake sooner than you would in your family car. Remember that you have a heavy load to stop now. Don't follow too closely. Learn to anticipate the other drivers even more than you do in normal driving situations. Allow plenty of time to stop.

Hook the trailer lights to the car. Driving without lights is hazardous during the night or day.

Check your hitch connection each and every time you get out of your car. Hitches have been known to work loose. There is the possibility that someone could tamper with it while you are away from the vehicle, too. Make it a habit to walk around the trailer checking all door and compartment latches and the hitch every time you are ready to drive away.

Don't expect circumstances to be such that you will always be in a position to turn around. Learn to back up. Practice makes perfect.

Traveling vacations with a horse can be most rewarding. But it is always best to make the plans for him prior to leaving. A child, small dog, or mother-in-law fit into normal vacation plans pretty well, but a horse can pose many problems along the way. Contact the chamber of commerce of the towns in which you wish to stay. Find out what the stabling and feed situation is.

This veteran traveler is wearing the latest in matching blanket and shipping boots.

There are regulations for interstate travel. Usually a health certificate is required in order to cross state lines. This is obtained through your local veterinarian. It is wise to carry your horse ownership papers and your trailer registration. The increase in horse thefts has made this necessary.

Don't make the horse travel nonstop over many hundreds of miles. He will need some rest. It is no easy job to stand up in a swaying, ever-moving vehicle. Try it yourself and see. Of course it is against the law for a person to ride in a vehicle that is being towed, but perhaps you could get the feel of it on your own driveway or on a secluded dirt road.

Some horses will not urinate while in the trailer. Allow your traveling horse a break. Some fresh air, relaxation, and water from time to time will refresh him greatly.

Now let's learn to unload a horse with a minimum of trouble and danger. Untie the halter rope first. Next, open the door. Unfasten the butt chain last. Stand to the side and be ready to grasp the lead rope as he finishes his exit from the trailer.

If he won't come out, pull gently on his tail or push on his chest from the manger door.

A horse who has been in a trailer for a long time will be stiff. Never

113

Even a short trail ride can be fun.

ask for strenuous work from him until he has had plenty of time to limber up and work out the kinks.

If your trailer does not have outside tie rings, by all means, have some installed. The rings in the manger may work to tie the horse that is outside, but the swinging manger door could cause a dangerous situation. Also the front of the trailer is not as safe of a place to tie as is the back.

An occasional horse will come out of the trailer looking like he went through World War I, even after a short ride. If your horse climbs the walls, steps on his own feet, and makes a mess out of himself in general, try using leg wraps. Buy cotton batting and wrap it around the legs with Ace bandages. Envelope the legs from just below the hocks to the top of the hooves. These wraps need to be fairly snug without cutting off circulation.

There are many schools of thought regarding the horse that is a poor traveler. One is that he needs more room. Cutting away part of, or removing, the divider is sometimes a solution that works. If you need to haul two horses, however, you may still have a problem.

Some trainers will drive a poor traveler down a bumpy road. After many planned quick stops and starts and bumps the horse will sometimes learn to balance himself better.

My seventeen-year-old daughter had a horse with that problem. The

114

mare never seemed to have enough room, even though our trailer was extra high and extra wide. If we wrapped her legs she'd step all over the other horse that traveled with her. After babying her along for three years, sometimes making extra trips so that we could always haul her alone, my daughter got thoroughly disgusted with her. The mare, then eight, was loaded into the trailer one day. She immediately fell to one side. Terri got a buggy whip out and swatted the horse's rump a few times. The mare stood up. Once again before we even started the car, she fell down for no reason. Terri "spanked" her until she stood up.

As we drove to the show, Terri asked me to stop about three times. Whenever Blessed lost her balance Terri got out and spanked her again. This scolding seemed to have solved our problem with Blessed. From that day to this, that mare has never again needed her legs wrapped. Neither have any of her riding companions.

If you just aren't able to handle a trailering problem yourself, don't be afraid to seek the aid of an expert. If your horse travels consistently poorly or won't enter the trailer without a fight, contact the services of a good trainer. He can sometimes accomplish in four days what you would never get done in ten years.

9 RIDING IN THE BACK COUNTRY

People are returning to nature, and it is only fitting that the horse enthusiast take along his treasured mount. Camping and backpacking have become enormously popular within the past few years. But horsepacking has even more to offer the adventuresome. There is that companionship between rider and horse, that wonderful feeling of closeness that cannot be matched in any other phase of riding. It is a matter of horse working for human and human caring for horse. Crossing the wilderness on horseback is certainly a team effort. And when each member of the team trusts and respects the other, the feeling is indescribable.

One gets a definite feeling of adventure as he treads on ground that few have dared tread. He feels a great sense of accomplishment as he conquers treacherous spots on the trail. He might choke up a little as he scans vast valleys from his perch on a mountaintop.

It is true that muscles get achey, dust and dirt become a part of everyday life, the work is endless, sometimes the weather is bad, and the bear tracks one sees might tend to spook a person. But when he catches a glimpse of a doe and her spotted fawn calmly grazing in the quiet of the hazy dawn, he knows that somehow it is all worthwhile.

There are numerous types of campers and styles of camping. In this chapter I will not be talking about motor home or house trailer camping. I won't even mention camping in designated campgrounds— you know, the ones that are complete with the luxury of a barbecue pit, picnic tables, and rest rooms. This chapter is not for those who wish to live a relaxing few days in the foothills behind their homes. So I won't even explain how to run an extension cord so a person can watch television, or shave with an electric razor each day.

This chapter is for those who want to horsepack in the back country—those who desire their own sort of romance with Mother Nature and her beautiful untrampled world.

Following on these pages are over sixty hints, ideas, and rules that you may or may not already know about horsepacking.

Relaxation is a real luxury for a horsepacker. One soon learns to appreciate every opportunity to stretch out and rest. It is not only the work involved with this mode of travel that so quickly tires a person. It is also the constant movement, the unrelenting action that your body must deal with every minute you are in the saddle. It's the decision you are faced with when you find a segment of trail has been washed down the side of the mountain, or when you find that the river you must cross is running higher and faster than you had imagined. It's all of this and more that causes that wonderful exhausted feeling at the end of each day and lures you to push on and to return again and again.

The first important step in horsepacking is to have the right horse. Agility in difficult terrain is not inborn. It is learned. Not all horses can cope with steep, mountainous trails. One that has been raised on the flat land is not a mountain horse.

Many people who raise horses don't realize the importance of exposing their young ones to uneven, sloping, open areas to improve their balance, agility, and coordination. As a foal is growing and developing he should also be given the opportunity to be learning.

We once had a horse that had been raised in a stall. From the time he was born until we got him at age five, he had never been allowed to run in a flat pasture, let alone learn to get to his footing on uneven ground. We took this horse on several short trail rides in a variety of terrain and found him to be hopelessly void of common trail sense. He could not even follow the widest trail without problems.

Switch backs were his real downfall. It seemed as though he would walk right off of the edge of a cliff if his rider didn't rein him around in the direction of the trail.

Stumbling was another problem this horse had. He was so used to the soft, flat ground in his stall, that he could not walk without stumbling. He misjudged distance and height as he tried to step over rocks. He didn't know how to handle ruts, ditches, or logs that were in his path. He was not trailwise.

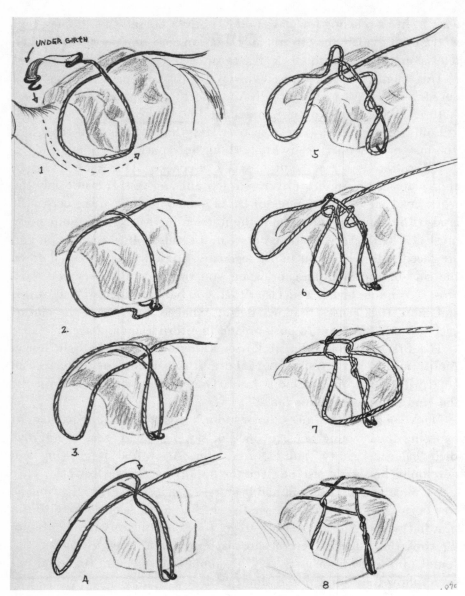

Diamond hitch.

To further stress the necessity of using only experienced or trailwise horses in the back country let me tell you about Snip. He was a backyard horse. He had spent most of his life in the same general area. He had probably always been a backyard horse. It was obvious that he had been trailered seldom, if ever. This indicated to us that he had seen few mountain trails.

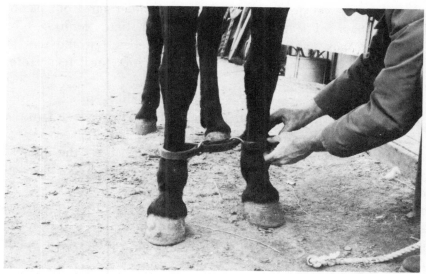

This is the proper way to put on hobbles.

One summer Snip was elected to go with three veteran hunting horses into extremely rugged country. Since he had been pampered and loved by his owners and had not been made to perform major feats of any kind, he soon became tired and impatient with the long, hard trip across a craggy ridge.

He started acting up, which usually got him his way at home. His rider dismounted, thinking he could lead Snip to a less precarious spot. But the horse pulled back and lost his footing completely. Snip tumbled head over hooves down the mountain side. The saddle bags were torn in half by the jagged rocks and their contents were strewn in many directions. His bridle was ruthlessly jerked from his head as he continued bouncing and rolling over and over again. He finally rested in a heap on the floor of a 300-yard deep canyon.

It wasn't until six days later that a very scarred, scratched, bruised, and sore Snip was finally walked out of the place that almost claimed his life.

The trail horse should be easy to catch. There are few things more annoying than trying to track down a runaway horse in thousands of acres of forest land.

The horse should stand tied without pulling back, fidgeting, or otherwise causing problems.

He should hobble. A horse that is hobbled can move around to graze, but can't usually get up enough speed to wander far from camp. Hobbles are made of leather, rawhide, and sometimes gunnysack or rope. There are any number of homemade varieties. I would suggest that you purchase a sturdy pair of hobbles at your local feed store. They are not expensive.

It is best to familiarize your horse with the hobbling process before you leave on your trip. To prevent an accident the first time or two the hobbles are used, you might stand the horse on a grassy area.

Fasten the hobbles around both front legs just above the fetlock. There will be a section of strap running between the two legs that will make the hobbles take on a figure-eight design.

Because of the many unfamiliar noises and objects that one comes across unexpectedly on a trail ride, the disposition of a trail horse should be calm. A flighty horse that is easily spooked could cause major havoc on a narrow trail.

He should also be eager, willing, and sound. If in doubt as to his soundness, call in a trained veterinarian for his opinion.

Many professionals agree that an ideal packhorse is short backed. He has a thick body and strong, sturdy legs. His backbone should be prominent and he should possess high withers. He must be fairly agile, because it takes more ability and stress to maneuver dead weight over tricky spots than live weight. The riding horses have a load that will move and redistribute the weight to aid them through difficult areas. The pack animal does not have this advantage.

The packhorse should have a level head. He must be sensible and able to keep his cool in many situations. There are instances when the pack boxes get hung up in narrow passages. Sometimes the whole outfit slips to one side and the contents are strewn along the trail or even down the side of a steep hill.

Do not take a young horse on a strenuous pack trip. Until he reaches the age of five or six he lacks the stamina needed to keep up with the group. Twice I have seen this warning disregarded. One young gelding became colicky and had to be walked most of the night. The other one was a filly. She became so exhausted, despite the group's frequent rest stops for her benefit, that she had to be taken home.

When you have the right horse for the trip, it is imperative that he be in good condition. Plan to work him every day for at least a month. This will not only help him, but it will be good for his rider. If possible ride in terrain similar to that which you will be experiencing on the trip.

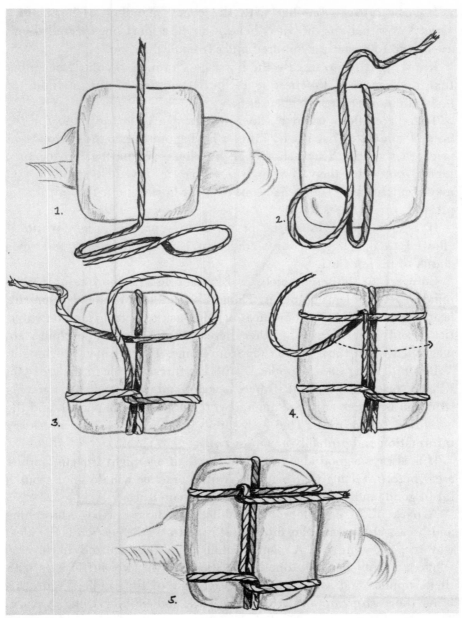

Box hitch.

It is best to be familiar with the overall handling of horses in a variety of situations, because, believe me, the most unexpected things are bound to occur one hundred miles from civilization.

Know what to do in case the horse gets a touch of colic. Remember that prevention is the best medicine. If unsure of the methods of prevention, refer back to chapter 5.

There are times when a shoer will trim a little too close for the horse's comfort. That is why I prefer having our horses shod two weeks prior to the trip. There should be no chance of having him become tender-footed by then. If your trip will cover very rocky ground, you may want to have Teflon pads put on your horse's feet. These will help prevent stone bruises.

If a shoe comes loose, be prepared to repair it, or remove it. If allowed to dangle, the horse could catch it on something and rip a chunk of his hoof off.

Contrary to the serene picture of a trail ride a person treasures in his mind's eye, problems do occur. Things like sunburn, broken equipment, lack of game or fish for food, heat or rain, lack of grazing land or water, ticks, and other crawly, slithery creatures. All of these things are magnified when they happen far from home. That's called roughing it.

Before leaving on a trip check with the forest service in the area you will be traveling. Find out if there is water and where, what the grazing situation is, which areas are open, if you will need a fire permit, and the condition of the trails. They will supply your party with all necessary information and probably a map or two.

It is always a good idea to take a couple of overnight trips in familiar areas before starting that big one. A little practice will do your group a lot of good, and you'll be having fun while you learn.

A pack outfit complete with saddle, pack boxes or bags, breeching and breast collar, and the thirty-foot rope to tie the gear on is the ideal way to pack your gear. A regular saddle can also be utilized. In the case where a family has only one horse, they can fill two duffle bags with their supplies and secure them on each side of the saddle. To do this bring the stirrups up and around the pack and tie everything in place. The family can still enjoy their backpack trip. The horse is doing the packing for them and they only have to walk.

Each horse should be outfitted with a set of saddlebags. Large canvas bags can be purchased at Army surplus stores and can be used as extra carryalls, or they can be made into saddlebags. A packer friend told me that a surplus store is a packer's heaven.

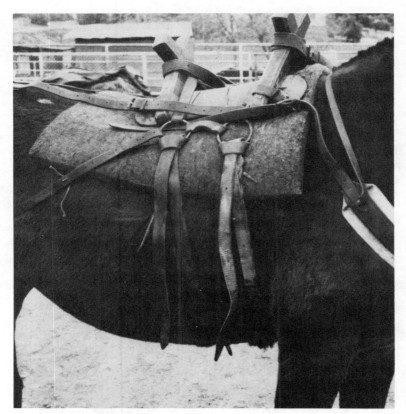

Basic pack saddle.

Pack saddle with pannier.

Duffle bag put on top (top packing).

Covered with weather and dustproof covering (diamond hitch).

The breeching is very important in mountain travel for the pack animal as well as for the riding horses.

It is wise to walk your horse before mounting if he is unaccustomed to the feel of saddlebags.

Supplies for an overnight trip will fit into saddlebags and can be carried by the horse that is being ridden. It is for longer trips that a packhorse will be necessary. Also, the more people in the group, the more packhorses you will need. By the same token, the more packhorses you have, the more of them you'll need to help carry their feed.

The checklist for a pack trip is similar to that of a camping trip after you have crossed off two-thirds of the items.

If it is necessary to haul part or all of the feed for the horses, consider the most nutritious types that are also easy to haul. Hay, for instance, would be most awkward to carry. Many experienced packers use alfalfa pellets, oats, or grain to supplement any available grazing. Again I caution you to get the horses used to any change in feed gradually before leaving home.

Due to the nature of the excursion, do not plan for your horse to gain weight. Everyone will come back from a pack trip with less flesh. Even you.

Each rider should have at least one canteen. Even if water is reported to be plentiful, always haul some in. If flowing streams are few, fill all containers every time you come to one. Those one-gallon plastic milk containers with handle and screw cap are handy to use for water. Note: water weighs about eight pounds to the gallon.

125

A feed bag is a convenient and efficient way to feed grain to your horse when away from home.

Grain is not wasted when fed to the horses by means of a feed bag. They are inexpensive and easy to pack in a small space.

Pellets can be fed off of the saddle pads. Remember to brush them thoroughly before using them under the saddle.

Be sure to take a sleeping bag that is suited to the climate. If the snow is still melting on the mountain peaks, you might need a warmer bag than you'd need in desert land during a heat wave. If your bedroll is to be carried behind your saddle, try rolling it up without first folding it in half. By rolling it tight it will not be so high that you can't get a leg over your saddle to mount. The bag will hang down along the horse's sides. The bedroll is apt to become saturated with the horse's sweat, so you might want to further protect it by tying a section of waterproof canvas around it.

A tarp can serve a variety of purposes. It is a ground cover, protection from the rain, and it can be used to help keep the dirt out of the pack boxes.

Each horse should be fitted with a heavy horsehair pad (the packhorse may require two) and bridle that are in good repair. Breast collars and breeching (to go around the rump) are a must for use on the pack animals and should be part of the riding horse's gear also. These heavy straps keep the saddle in place in hilly areas.

126

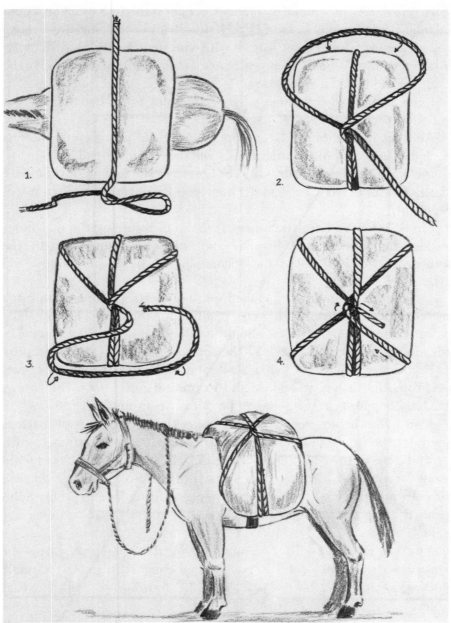

Squaw hitch.

A repair kit for leather equipment is important to have. This could include a leather punch, extra latigo, thin strips of rawhide, and a small roll of bailing wire. You will have with you one of nature's own repair kits: your horse's tail. Use a few braided strands of horsehair to fix the bridle or saddle in an emergency.

Remember to include some of your grooming tools. Use them before and after each day's ride.

Another hint is to start the trip with a clean pad. Before saddling each day scrape all of the dried sweat and hair from the pad.

Include a good wound dressing for horses, in the first-aid kit. Because the horses draw flies even more than you do, include, also, an insect repellent.

Check into the latest treatment techniques regarding the poisonous snakes and insects that live in your area. Be equipped with the knowledge to administer the recommended treatment calmly and efficiently.

Lamb's wool should be included on the check list. Pieces of this soft material are used to provide extra padding for the horses where saddle sores might occur. The horse should be thoroughly checked every day for any tender or raw areas and the sores should be treated promptly.

Each horse will need a halter, lead rope, and either hobbles or a long, soft rope that is big enough around to prevent rope burns. This rope is for tethering, or tying him long so he can move around and graze.

Flat, nylon halters are nice to use under the bridle. If a rope halter is used, let the headstall of the bridle out one notch to make a better fit.

You'll need a wide-brimmed hat with a chin tie. I usually take an old straw Western hat and poke two holes at the base of the crown on each side. I run a piece of ribbon or a heavy shoestring through these holes from the top. I can either tie it at the back of my head or under my chin.

You can make do with a minimum of regular camp gear. Leave the fancy heaters, tents (unless you're expecting rain), cots, portable potties, vanity sets, lawn chairs, and the four-burner cook stove at home.

Take along a lantern only if there is room. Pack Sterno heat to cook with for those times when you aren't planning to build a fire. Take only a minimum of cooking and eating utensils. One pan to boil water for coffee, instant cereal, and for washing dishes, a frying pan, spatula and wooden spoon for serving and stirring, one spoon and a wide-mouth cup per person to be used as a drinking vessel, and a bowl should be all you really need.

Polly is packed and ready for the trip. Note the diamond on the top of the pack. This is the diamond hitch.

Of course you'll know to include a warm jacket for those chilly nights, a sharp pocket knife, flashlight with extra bulbs, and batteries as you always do on a camping trip.

The canned meals such as spaghetti, stew, and raviolis can be heated in their cans. Always remove the lid before heating.

I can't even try to make out a complete menu that will suit everyone. Some insist on steak every night and figure out a way to carry an ice chest to keep the meat from spoiling. Others spend many hours a day cooking gourmet meals because that is the thing they enjoy most about camping in the wilderness. For the horsepacker who is limited in space and doesn't want to spend a lot of time cooking, I suggest taking a minimum of high-protein foods: hard cheeses, jerky, fresh and dried fruits, fairly uncrushable breads such as pita, rye, and sourdough, canned sardines, tuna, instant cereals in individual packets, and other such convenience foods like the dehydrated ones you find in sporting-goods stores.

Load the pack boxes so that nothing rattles. Not only does it unnerve the horse to hear a noise coming from the pack, but the looser the items are packed, the more likely they are to be broken or mangled.

Wrap glass items in several thicknesses of newspaper to insulate them against breakage.

Fill the boxes and saddlebags as the box boy at your local market

129

does. Heavy things go on the bottom, crushable items should be protected between or on top of sturdier objects. You might have noticed that the box boy will not pack cleaning items such as soap powder and bleach in the same bag with the food. Consider this in arranging your pack load. Fumes from a nonfood item could interfere with the flavor of the food. Spilled chemical products would cause even more problems.

Fill the pack boxes while they are on the ground. Never try to put them on the horse first.

A loaded pack outfit should not weigh more than 150 pounds. The weight is usually distributed like this: 50 pounds on each side and fifty pounds on top.

If the pack boxes are not loaded so that they weigh exactly the same, the load will slip to one side of the horse and he could eventually lose it.

Carry a small scale with you on your trip so that you will be sure that the boxes are always packed evenly.

Once you have your riding horse saddled, and the saddlebags and bedroll are secured, walk him around for a few minutes before mounting. He may need time to get used to the strange feel of the extra dead weight.

Horsepacking is done at a walk. Never expect a packhorse or a heavily loaded riding horse to trot. Not only is it hard on him to have the heavy weight slapping him with every bouncy step, but you may find, at the end of a trot, that your eggs are already scrambled for your next morning's meal.

Plan to cover a maximum of about fifteen miles a day. A horse walks about two-and-a-half to three miles an hour.

The packhorse will have to be led part of the time. Use a fifteen-foot rope. Never tie it to the saddle horn. Either hold it in your hand or take a dally or two around the horn so that it will slide off if an emergency should occur. Watch that the rope doesn't get caught under the riding horse's tail. Some good pack horses will follow closely behind without being led.

Some horses will rest when tired, but if yours doesn't, you will have to stop him for a breather from time to time. This is especially true while climbing a steep incline. Come to a dead stop every forty to fifty feet for eight to ten seconds. You might turn him perpendicular to the incline so that he is in a more comfortable position to rest.

Every few hours dismount, loosen the cinch, raise the saddle and

Lay blankets and pads wet side up on "resting" saddle. This will allow them to dry out.

blanket, and allow the cool air to pass over the horse's back. This will aid in preventing saddle galls.

When stopping for a lunch or rest break, unsaddle the horses and let them rest, too. Always lay the saddle and hang the bridles out of reach of the horses. Put the pads wet side up so they can dry out a little.

A tired, winded horse will begin to stumble. This could cause a dangerous situation for everyone. Don't let the horses get that tired. When a horse does stumble, don't jerk the reins. Let him catch his balance by giving him his head.

This is good advice to follow in complicated terrain, also. The horse can usually pick his way better than his rider can. Don't rush him.

While riding uphill rise up out of the saddle slightly to get the weight off of the horse's back. Don't hang way over the neck, however. While moving downhill place your body at a more perpendicular angle to the horse. Place your weight over his center of gravity and use light contact with his mouth. Let him see where he is putting his feet.

Sometimes it is possible to climb or descend a hill by zigzagging across the face of it rather than going in a straight line from the top to the bottom and vice versa. Gradually work your way up and down by moving at an angle and back and forth.

It takes practice for a packhorse to learn to judge the width of his

It's easier on your horse if you zigzag up and down hills rather than working in a straight line.

load. He will usually suffer bruised hips and sore ribs caused by contact between the boxes and protruding rocks or trees. But soon he will learn to avoid the pain, and the boxes won't acquire any more nicks and scrapes either.

Load the packhorse as the last act before leaving camp each morning, and make sure to unload him first each evening. Do not make him stand around for long periods with the heavy pack on.

HORSE FIRST ALWAYS!!

Selection of the camp for the evening usually depends on availability of grazing land for horses. If grazing area is subject to frost during the night, set up camp early in the afternoon so that the horses can graze long enough before the frost sets in.

If water supply is low, water the horses once during the day and let them get their fill at night. They won't drink as much water when they are cool.

Sometimes the trees will offer a means of making a corral. Tie ropes around available trees to contain horses.

The ropes I speak of that should be brought in with you have many uses. Another one is to get firewood. If the log is very large, tie a rope around it and drag the log from horseback into camp.

Keep leather away from mice and all equipment away from ants. The saddles should be stored for the night off of the ground. Beware of trees with those big ants swarming in them, though.

Don't show off or take unnecessary chances in the back country. It is a long way from civilization to hazard a serious injury.

If a horse should slip and tumble several hundred feet to the bottom of a mountain, quick action will be necessary. Hike down to him. If the saddle and bridle are still on, take them off any way you can. They could be restricting his breathing. Don't hesitate to cut a cinch when it comes to your horse's life. Just about all there is to do at this point is to wait. If he is down, help him to get into a comfortable position while he relaxes and tries to get his breath back.

When he starts to stir and seems to want to get up, help him to his feet. Check him over for cuts, abrasions, and broken bones. Survey his condition as best you can. Is the horse strong enough to climb out? If not, will a few days rest help the situation?

Sometimes a shock such as this will traumatize the horse so he can't mentally or physically manage to walk, even on flat ground. Climbing out of a deep canyon is out of the question at this point. If this is the case, you will have to help the horse gain his strength by supplying him with the best in feed and water and by letting him rest. He should be encouraged to do some exercising each day as he grows stronger. Shelter from the weather, water, good feed and rest will be his immediate needs.

To help a horse out of a bad situation like this, it may be necessary to cut a trail by hand for him to follow out. Use the zigzag method if the mountainside is very steep.

People who travel in the wilderness sometimes forget how far they really are from civilization. When an accident occurs, help can be extremely hard to get. In the case of an injured horse, help is almost nonexistent from agencies if you are too deep into the back country.

Yes, you are pretty much on your own when you leave the city, so plan to be as self-sufficient as you can and don't take chances that could spell trouble to you or your animals.

Try to set up camp during the daylight hours.

The evening camp procedure will go something like this: Unload the packhorse and brush him down. Then unsaddle the riding horses. Make sure that all animals are cooled out and then either tether or hobble them where they can graze.

After your evening meal, give the horses their ration of feed. Water them and then put them away for the night.

The horses should be tied to a solid object within your view and not within kicking distance of their equine friends.

Tie the horses with a quick-release knot. Never allow the lead or the tie rope to become knotted. Imagine how hard it would be to untie a rope that is knotted in several places.

Keep a flashlight handy in case there is a need for you to jump to untangle or catch a loose horse.

Do not wash utensils or yourself in streams. Carry all wash water away from the stream to use it. Our streams and rivers are highly contaminated in many areas of our country. Let's not add to this problem.

Carry out everything that won't burn to ashes. Crush tin cans and carry them out, too. It used to be accepted to bury litter; however, in some places that practice has been outlawed.

The new accepted rule is to carry everything out that you brought in.

By the same token, don't leave pop tops, broken glass, tin can lids, or any other litter like this. These things not only cause a messy wilderness, they also endanger our wildlife.

It is we who are intruding in their world; let's leave it as we found it, safe and beautiful for the animals, for other people, and for ourselves.

10 THE HOW-TO CHAPTER

Western equipment and attire can be expensive. If you have a basic knowledge of sewing, you can cut down on the cost considerably by making many of the items yourself.

This chapter is not intended to be a lesson in sewing. It is to be used as a guide by those who can already sew. Numerous hints and tips are added to prevent that trial-and-error phase we all must usually endure when trying something new.

SHIRT OR JACKET

Let's start with a Western shirt for either a man or a woman. There are many Western-style shirt and blouse patterns on the market these days. It is not always necessary, however, to purchase a new pattern. If you have a shirt pattern that fits well and is becoming to your particular figure, make it look Western. Here's how:

When you buy the fabric, purchase a scant one-quarter yard more than the pattern calls for.

When cutting the fabric, lay the top part of the shirt back pattern on a piece of newspaper, or better yet a heavier paper such as a brown paper market bag. With a pencil, draw around the neck, shoulder, and armhole of the pattern. Next, cut on these lines.

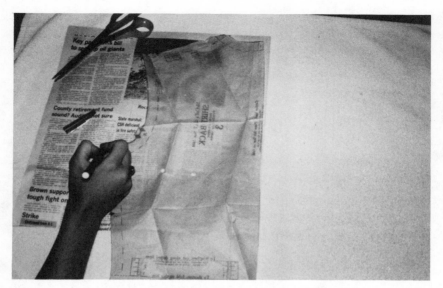

Fold the paper in half so that the armholes are together, and draw the design you want your yoke to have. Cut away excess.

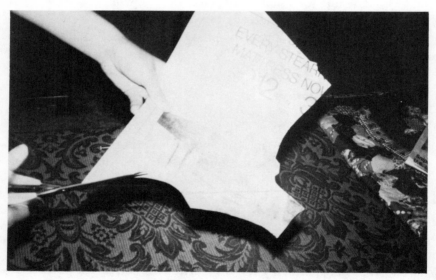

Do the same thing for the fronts of the shirt. The front yokes should have the same basic design as the back, only smaller. They will not extend as far down as the back does either.

If you wish, you can add a pointed shape to the pockets. A design similar to the one you choose for the yokes can also be given to the sleeves or cuffs.

Lay the yoke patterns on the fabric, and cut them out as you do the shirt pieces.

The yoke should be sewn on before starting the shirt. Press the raw edges of the curved part of the yokes under 5/8 inch. Pin yoke to the back matching neck and armhole edges. Stitch 1/4" from the turned-under yoke edges.

These directions can also be applied to a jacket pattern.

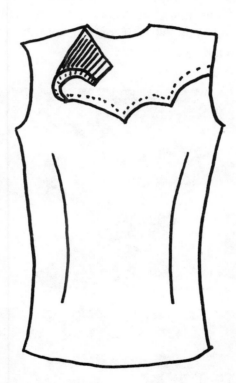

EQUITATION SUIT

A lot of girls in the West wear equitation suits in shows. These suits are made of a fabric that will give slightly with the body movements. They are made to fit the body rather snugly. The less loose material there is to blow and flop around, the smoother the horse will seem as he performs.

These suits usually consist of a body suit and matching or coordinating slacks.

The fabric for equitation suits is predominantly polyester knit. Some ready-made suits are done in woven fabric such as cotton blends. The stretch materials provide a much better fit, however.

It is important, before making an equitation suit, to consider the size and figure of the girl who will be wearing it. Judges are probably not particularly fashion conscious, but the overall appearance is definitely important.

A heavy girl should stay away from busy or loud prints. The design of her suit should be simple and uncluttered. Pockets should be eliminated. Don't add fancy buttons. Make the yokes plain with a rather long line to them. The fit of an equitation suit should not be quite as snug on a heavy person.

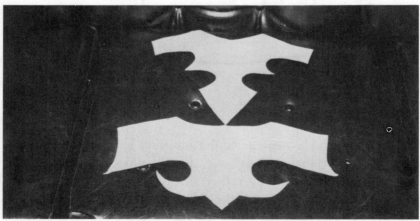

A very slim girl can wear the wilder designs in fabric. She can wear pockets if they are in correct proportion to her size. She should choose a wide yoke style to give width to her back. The fancier yoke designs are alright for this person.

The equitation suit pants can be made from any good fitting pant pattern with an elastic waistband. When cutting out the pants, taper them slightly at the knee so that they will be more fitted. Then they may be flared out to the hem.

If you desire a stitched crease in the front pants legs, do it before you put them together.

Sew pants as usual until you get to the waistband. Make the casing and insert the elastic.

For the belt loops, cut eight pieces of matching fabric approximately 4" x 1½". At one end of each piece cut the corners so that there is a point that is centered.

Using two of these sections, sew them right sides together, along both long ends and around the point, leaving open the other end. Do this with all belt loop sections. Turn to the right side and press. You now have four lined belt loops.

Next, position the loops on the pants waist with two in the front and two in the back. Make sure they are placed evenly. Stitch them as the diagram shows, allowing the loops to extend slightly above the pants line. In this way the belt will cover the top edge of the pants.

The four-belt-loop style is for those who have a Western belt with their name across the back. If this is not the case with you, you may want to add a fifth loop at center back. If you do, I suggest you move the other two back loops toward the sides slightly.

You need not worry about the polyester raveling. Simply turn your raw edges, hem, and so forth, one time. This will prevent a bulky look.

Hems can be done by machine. Don't bother to add cuffs on pants legs. The chaps will hide all of your extra effort anyway.

The equitation body suit can easily be made from any regular shirt pattern that has a rounded shirt tail. Following the diagram, cut curves for the legs on the front section and add the panty extender to the back section.

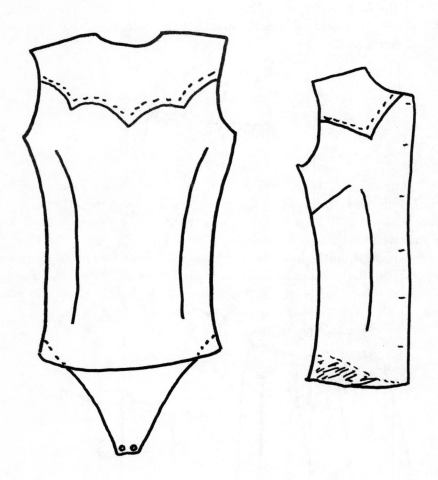

If you don't want to add the bulk of the double thickness at the yoke of your Western shirt, you can use pin tucking, decorative braid or trim, or a fancy machine stitch.

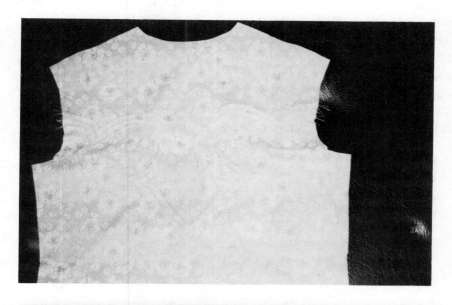

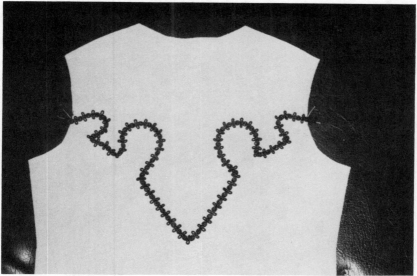

To do this you draw your yoke design on the shirt back and fronts with chalk. Then follow the lines to acquire the look you want. This is a great idea for your summer outfit. Without the bulk of extra fabric it is much cooler and more comfortable.

Some people add a contrasting shade of piping to accent the outline of a double yoke.

If you have created a rather intricate design for a yoke, you might have less trouble utilizing it with this method. Put right sides together and following the detailed edge, stitch a piece of pellon which was cut to match the yoke design to the yoke. Clip your corners, curves, etc., as you always do and then turn and press the piece. Now when you sew the yoke on you have no raw edges to contend with. The pellon is practically invisible even if it should slide into view.

The collar of the equitation suit has to cover a tie. If you cut it so that it comes to a point at center back, your tie will not show.

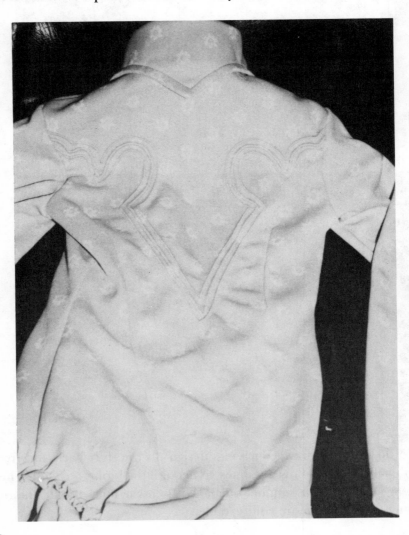

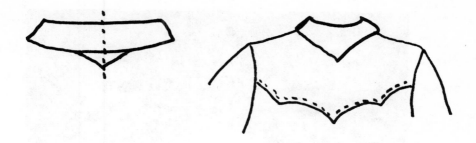

Topstitching is one thing that gives Western clothing that Western look. Do not sew too close to the edge. Topstitch about ¼" from the edge to give a nicer, more professional look to your clothes.

Use either an invisible zipper or buttons down the front of the body suit.

There is a way to put the zipper in so that the yokes meet in the right place in front. Stitch one side of the zipper to the front. Then zip up the zipper and pin it to the other side at the point where the yokes should meet in front. Unzip it and, with a basting stitch, sew about 1½" along where it is pinned. Check again to see if zipped, the yokes meet at the right place. If so, finish stitching the entire zipper.

Flat snap fasteners will work for the crotch of the body suit.

Put elastic in the legs, but don't make it too tight.

You may want to use a regular body suit pattern. If so, remember to consider the convenience to the wearer if the opening is in front. To alter a pattern that has a back opening, cut the back on the fold. To make the back fit nicely, put darts on both sides of center back.

CHAPS

Chaps cost around $75 to over $100 to buy. Why not make your own and save $40 or more?

The first step, of course, is to find an outlet that sells the dyed and tanned hides. Many places will sell ½ hides and that is about what you will need for one pair of chaps. If they are for a very small child you could get two pair out of ½ hide.

Fabric stores carry many new synthetic materials that resemble leather. Some of them are quite suitable for chaps.

Chap patterns are usually available at places that sell leather.

If you can't find a pattern, borrow a pair of chaps to use as a guide in making yours.

Even with a pattern you will need to have the correct measurements of the person who will wear the chaps. For show, the chaps should be very fitted. For the trail they needn't be.

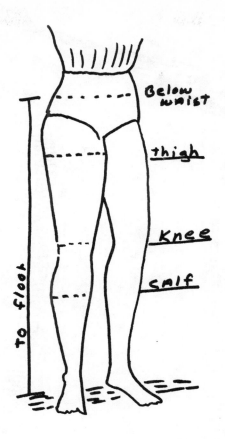

Measure around the hips, just below the belt. Measure around the highest point of the thigh, the knee, the calf, and the length you will want the chaps. They should go to the floor in the front and they will angle off and drag the foor at the fringe.

Lay each leg pattern right side up on the hide. Draw with chalk around the pattern that has been cut or folded to the correct measurements. Allow six to eight inches for the fringe.

Cut two thicknesses of the belt sections.

With the chaps as a guide, put your pieces together and glue them in place. Separate the zippers and glue them in place on the legs. The zippers should start at the top and zip down the leg as far as they will reach. They will zip up to open the chaps.

Now either use your own heavy-duty sewing machine or ask your local shoe-repair man to stitch the chaps as they are glued.

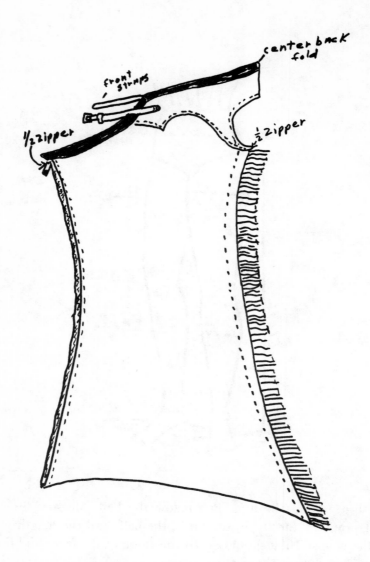

front straps

center back fold

½ zipper

½ zipper

Buy silver or brass buckles to secure the chaps in the front; they will be solid across the waist back.

Add silver nameplates, conchos, or initials as you can afford them. They make very nice gifts.

CARING FOR YOUR CHAPS

To care for your chaps, always fold or hang them wrong side out when they are not being used. This is especially important at the horse show. The dust won't cling to the smooth side as it will to the rough one.

A plastic cover will keep them cleaner whether they are in storage or on their way to a show.

Wear them only when you need to. I don't mean you should take them off between classes. Don't put them on until your first class is nearly ready to start and take them off after the last one of the day.

If you get off of your horse, roll the chaps up so that they don't drag in the dirt.

No matter what precautions you take, the chaps are bound to get dirty sooner or later. If they are true cowhide you can wash them. Either hose them off on a cement patio or walkway using soap and a brush to scrub the bad spots, or toss them into the washing machine.

If you chose the machine method, remove all metal pieces. Use warm or cold water, never hot. Don't let the chaps spin through the whole spin cycle. Take them out while they are still fairly wet. Scrape the excess water out of the leather with your hand. Pull and stretch the chaps in every direction to help them get their shape back and then lay them in the *shade* over a padded fence or pipe or some other object that won't leave a crease in the leather.

You might stretch the chaps again as they dry. If they are too tight, put them on while they are still damp. If you bend in them a few times they will stretch out a little more.

A word of caution. Never put chaps in the dryer. You'll end up with nothing but a stiff, wrinkled, glob of dried out leather.

Some chap colors fade much more quickly than others. If the original shade was a fairly common color, it is possible to brighten the chaps with dye.

After washing the chaps, fill the machine tub ¼ full with water. Mix the dye with a quart of water (or as directed on the package) and add to the water in the machine. Let the chaps agitate in the dye for a few minutes and then spin the excess water from the tub.

Some people do not rinse the dye completely out. They claim it gives a richer shade if you don't.

In between these thorough washings you can clean mud, food, and other types of soil from the chaps with a damp scrub brush or rag.

When a person outgrows her chaps, she should not discard them. Sell them to someone who can wear them and have a head start toward the purchase of your next pair of show chaps.

HORSE BLANKETS

For an interesting gift for a person who loves his horse, buy a horse blanket and put the horse's name on it in big letters. We like to use iron-on tape to make the letters. The tape comes in a variety of colors and it adheres well to most blanket fabric.

To make a horse blanket you must know for what it will be used. If it is to discourage flies from biting the horse or to keep his hair from becoming bleached by the sun or even to protect his coat from dust, you could select a medium-weight denim, broadcloth, or a fairly heavy cotton.

If your purpose in making this blanket is to keep him dry when it is wet out, consider a vinyl or a waterproof oilcloth.

A warm night blanket might consist of heavy denim, canvas, or wool lined with fake fur.

The webbing for blankets, the D rings, blanket fasteners, etc. are all obtainable individually at the Western tack store. One friend of mine replaces all of the webbing on old blankets with lawn-chair webbing. She claims that it is a stronger material than the webbing sold for this purpose.

Borrow a blanket that fits your horse. Note any possible reasons for alteration and then use it as a pattern in making one for your horse.

Notice how the webbing is applied, where the fasteners are placed, and so forth.

If you ever intend washing the horse blanket, be sure to purchase fabric that is machine washable. The material must also be strong.

Don't short cut. If the store blanket has three rows of stitching, stitch yours three times too. If you scrimp on fabric, design, or time, you will be putting in more of each in repairs on the blanket.

LEG WRAPS (SHIPPING BOOTS)

Use cotton batting covered by an Ace bandage on each lower leg and reuse each time you trailer. As an alternative you can make leg wraps to match the blanket.

Measure the leg around. Then note the length from the hocks and knees to the hoof.

Buy fake fur and a heavy denim or vinyl to the measurements plus about three inches to overlap.

Line the fabric with one or two thicknesses of fake fur (depending on its weight).

Use Velcro strips to hold the wraps on the legs. This can be purchased at any yardage store.

SADDLE BLANKET

These can be made from just about any material. I've seen them made of the fake fur, polyester, denim, wool, and even yarn. Initials, tassels, or pom-poms can be added to individualize a blanket.

The color seems to be the most important thing to consider here. Choose one that will complement the rider's horse and clothes.

Use your favorite saddle pad as a guide and be sure that your finished product will cover it completely.

The loosely woven fabrics are best for saddle blankets. They give and contour to fit the back of a horse. A fabric of tight weave will buckle and wrinkle more.

TIES

There are many varieties of Western ties for show. They can be fashioned of the same leather that is used in the chaps, making a very smart outfit. The polyester of the equitation suit can also be used to make a matching tie.

You could use a softer, filmier fabric such as chiffon or nylon for a feminine look.

I like to take a section of chap leather and cut from it a strip that is 22" long and 1" wide. I cut the two ends at opposite angles and then I put it around the neck, cross it at the front, and secure it where it makes an X with a tie tack. Adjust the length for the individual.

Another simple leather tie is the little bib tie. Cut a piece of leather about 12" long and 1" wide at each end but graduating in width on one long side until it is about 3½" or 4" wide at this point in the very center of the piece. The widest part will form a point at center front.

Then to add a little reinforcement and design, cut some more leather to sew in layers along the pointed section.

Sew elastic on one end of the tie back and a snap on the other end and on the elastic. This will be at center back.

TOTE BAG

This unique little tote bag can be utilized in a number of ways, as a gym or athletic bag, overnight case, beach tote, traveling pouch, and it is a perfect size for carrying a nice set of show bridle and reins, chaps, gloves, registration papers, and other delicate show necessities.

This one is made of broadcloth. A vinyl, heavy canvas, or any other suitable fabric can be used.

Cut two circles of the fabric using a pie pan as a guide. Then take the measurement around your pie pan. Cut a third piece of fabric that measurement plus 1" x 25".

This is when you should embroider your name, or any other design you want, on the large piece of your tote.

Keep in mind that the opening will be at the top.

Stitch the narrow webbing to the large section of the fabric to make your carrying handles.

Next, sew the round ends to the main piece.

By purchasing an old jacket at the second-hand store, you may be able to get a heavy-duty zipper to use in your tote, for less then you would pay for it new. A long zipper is best, because it creates an opening of a size large enough so that you may easily find your gear inside the tote.

Insert the zipper.

This tote bag can make a perfect and inexpensive gift for a tennis player, track star, baseball player, fisherman, hunter, or for anyone. The size and fabric can be adjusted to the person and her needs.

LAP ROBE

After you have shown for some time and you have accumulated a couple of walls full of show ribbons, you may become frantic about what to do with all of them.

Here is one idea. Make them into a delightful and meaningful lap robe for your favorite spectator.

A lap robe would be about 3' x 3'. Buy a piece of muslin of that size. Lay it on the floor and begin placing all of the ribbons on it in a design of your choice.

Choose a square pattern and place ribbons longways along the edges. Work toward the center. Or make a sunburst design by starting in the middle and working out with the ribbons overlapping and fanning out toward the outer edges.

Plan your design according to color or just give it a patchwork look and mix the colors throughout.

Pin the ribbons in place and sew them on by machine. There is no need to turn under your ribbon edges, because they are already finished.

Stitch with red thread on red ribbons, yellow thread on yellow ribbons, and so forth.

If you wish to make this robe extra special, you might want to hand-embroider around each ribbon. I've seen this done in the same stitch and I've also seen people use a variety of stitches on the article.

Once the ribbons are sewn in place, choose a satin or cotton blend backing and baste it in place. Bind around all raw edges with blanket binding or the lap robe backing you've chosen.

There are many many more pieces of Western attire or horse gear that can be duplicated at home. Before purchasing an expensive item, look it over and decide if you could make one like it.

Don't make your decision hastily. Think about the time involved. Will this take too much time from other important duties? Will the materials be difficult or impossible to obtain in your neck of the woods? Will this be another of those projects you will most likely start and never finish?

Consider all of these factors and then decide.

Good luck and good horsemanship.

GLOSSARY

BACKYARD HORSE: One used and kept for pleasure.

BAREBACK RIDING: Riding without a saddle.

BARN-SOUR HORSE: Same as herd bound.

BARREL: The part of a horse between his shoulders and hips.

BIT: The metal part of the bridle that fits into the horse's mouth.

BOTS: Yellow specks (larva) that bot flies leave on the front legs and chest hairs of a horse.

BREAST COLLAR: The strap that fits around the horse's chest. This item is optional equipment with a saddle, but very useful for mountain riding.

BREECHING: The strap that fits around the saddled horse's rump. It is used for mountain riding and packing.

BRIDLE: Headstall, bit, and reins.

BRIDLE PATH: (1) Horse trail; (2) An area, just behind the ears, where the mane is shaved to make room for the headstall.

BRIDLING: The act of putting on the bridle.

BROKE HORSE: One that can be ridden.

BROOD MARE: Mare used for breeding.

BUTT BAR OR BUTT CHAIN: The sturdy bar or chain that snaps behind the animal in a horse trailer.

CANTER: An English term meaning a collected gallop.

CASTILE SOAP: A mild soap made from fats and oils and used on leather.

152

CATCH PEN: A small enclosure designed to help catch pasture horses.

CENTER DIVIDER: A divider in a horse trailer that separates the horses.

CHAPS: Leather leggings.

CHEEK PIECE: The part of a bit that runs along the horse's cheeks.

CHIN STRAP: Chain or leather strap on a bridle that fits under the chin.

CINCH: A wide, webbed girth that runs under the barrel of the horse to hold the saddle on.

CLUCKING: The clicking noise one makes with his mouth to move a horse on.

COLIC: An often fatal illness usually caused by improper feeding.

COLOR BREED: A breed recognized for a particular color pattern, such as Appaloosa, Pinto, etc.

COLT: Male horse under three years old.

CONCHO: A small metal (often silver) decoration on a Western saddle.

CONFORMATION: The build of a horse.

CORRAL: An enclosure in which horses or cattle are kept.

CRIBBING: Chewing on wood.

CURRY COMB: Rubber or metal device with rows of small teeth, used to groom a horse.

DAM: Mother horse.

DISMOUNT: To get off of a horse.

DUDE: Newcomer to the world of horses.

EASY KEEPER: A horse that gains weight easily.

ENDURANCE RIDE: An organized and carefully controlled contest in which the endurance of the horse is tested.

ENTRY NUMBER: A cardboard number that is worn by contestants in a horse show.

EQUESTRIAN: A person who rides a horse.

EQUINE: A horse.

EQUITATION: The art of horseback riding.

EQUITATION SUIT: Two-piece outfit worn in horse shows by women riders.

FARRIER: Horse shoer.

FEED BAG: A cloth bag from which a horse eats grain.

FILLY: A female horse under three years old.

FLOAT (TEETH): The act of filing jagged edges from a horse's teeth.

FOAL: A baby horse that isn't weaned.

GAIT: Sequence in which a horse puts his feet down. Walking is one gait, jogging another, etc.

GALLOP: Run.

GALLS: Sores on the horse caused by some part of the saddle or girth rubbing.

GELDING: Castrated male horse.

GRADE HORSE: One that can't be registered with any horse breed association.

GRAZING: Eating growing grass.

GREEN HORSE: One that is untrained.

GROOMING: Cleaning and brushing a horse.

GYMKHANA: Competition riding; speed events, games, and contests.

HALTER: A device that fastens around the horse's head for ease in leading, handling, or tying.

HALTER CLASS: An event at a horse show in which the handler leads rather than rides his horse. The horse is judged on conformation.

HANDS: A way of measuring a horse. One hand equals four inches.

HARD KEEPER: A horse that requires more feed.

HEAD SHY: A term used to describe a horse who does not like to have his head touched.

HEADSTALL: The part of the bridle that fits over the head of the horse.

HEALTH CERTIFICATE: A document the veterinarian issues on a healthy horse when he is to be taken out of state.

HERD BOUND: A term given a horse that doesn't like to leave his equine friends.

HOBBLES: Thick leg straps that fit around a horse's lower leg and keeps him from straying.

HOOF PICK: Hoof-cleaning device.

HORSE BLANKET: Blanket that covers the horse's body.

HORSE PACKING: Overnight wilderness traveling on a horse.

HORSE TRADER: One who buys and sells horses for a profit.

JOG: Western term for trot.

LATIGO: Straps that fasten the cinch to the saddle.

LEAD ROPE: A section of rope that snaps to the halter and enables the horse to be led.

LEATHER PUNCH: Device that punches holes in leather.

LEG UP: Getting help mounting. "Give me a leg up."

LEG WRAPS: Thick wrapping that protects a horse's legs while trailer traveling.

LONGE: A way of exercising a horse from the ground.

LONGE LINE: Thirty-foot rope used to longe a horse in a circle around the handler.

LOPE: Western term for a slow gallop.

MANE: Long hair on horse's neck.

MANE AND TAIL COMB: A metal or plastic comb for untangling mane and tail hairs.

MANGER: Feed bin.

MARE: Adult female horse.

MOUNT: (1) To get on a horse; (2) Term used for a riding horse.

MOUTHPIECE: The bar of a bit that fits into horse's mouth.

NEAR SIDE: Left side of the horse.

NEATS FOOT OIL: Used as a dressing for leather.

NECK REIN: To use pressure with the rein on the side of a horse's neck to cause him to turn.

NICKER: A throaty sound the horse makes to imply pleasure.

OFF FEED: Not eating.

OFF SIDE: The right side of a horse.

OUTLAW: Vicious horse.

PACK HORSE: One that carries a pack on overnight riding trips.

PACK SADDLE: A saddle specially designed to carry a pack outfit.

PLAY DAY: An informal horse show.

PLOW-REIN: To use the reins individually by pulling on the right rein for a right turn, etc.

POINTS: The black on the lower legs of a horse.

PONY: (1) A horse under 58 inches (14.2 hands) high; (2) To lead one horse while riding another.

PORTABLE CORRAL: One that can be moved from place to place.

PUREBRED: An animal of pedigree.

REINS: Leather straps the rider uses to guide the horse.

RIATA (REATA): A small lariat that is tied to the side of a Western saddle in competitive riding.

RIDING DOUBLE: Two people on the same horse.

ROAN: A coat of any color with white hairs throughout.

ROPE BURN: A sore caused by a rope scraping swiftly across the skin.

SADDLE BLANKET: Blanket that fits between the saddle and saddle pad.

SETTLED: (1) A term used for an older horse that is calm; (2) Pregnant.

SHANKS: Sides of the bit that hang downward from the mouthpiece.

SHOD: Wearing horse shoes.

SHOWMANSHIP: A show class performed at hand. The handler is judged on how he manages his horse.

SHY: To move quickly from an object that has frightened the horse.

SIDE-PASS: To move the horse sideways while astride him.

SIRE: A father horse.

SOUND: In good condition.

SPLIT EAR HEADSTALL: One that encloses one ear.

SPOOKED HORSE: Scared or excited horse.

SQUARED UP: To be squared up, a horse must be standing square with his weight equally distributed on all four feet.

STALLION: Adult male horse.

STOCK RACK: Wood or metal provisions for carrying horses or cattle in the back of a truck.

STOCK TRUCK: One that is designed to carry horses or cattle.

SWEAT SCRAPER: A metal device used to rid horse's hair of excess moisture.

SWITCHBACK: A hairpin curve on a road or trail.

TACK: Horse equipment.

TACK ROOM: Place where tack is stored.

TANDEM TRAILER: One with two sets of wheels.

TEATS: Mare's nipples.

TETHER: Tying a horse on a long rope so he can move around and graze.

TRAINER: One who trains horses and often gives riding lessons for a living.

VET CHECK: Examination by a veterinarian.

WEANLING: A weaned foal.

INDEX